A RUMOR ABOUT THE
JEWS

A RUMOR ABOUT THE
JEWS

ANTISEMITISM, CONSPIRACY, AND THE *PROTOCOLS OF ZION*

Stephen Eric Bronner

OXFORD
UNIVERSITY PRESS

OXFORD
UNIVERSITY PRESS

Oxford   New York
Auckland Bangkok Buenos Aires Cape Town Chennai
Dar es Salaam Delhi Hong Kong Istanbul Karachi Kolkata
Kuala Lumpur Madrid Melbourne Mexico City Mumbai Nairobi
São Paulo Shanghai Taipei Tokyo Toronto

First published by St. Martin's Press, LLC, 2000
First published as an Oxford University Press paperback, 2003
198 Madison Avenue, New York, New York, 10016

www.oup.com

Oxford is a registered trademark of Oxford University Press

Library of Congress Cataloging-in-Publication Data
Bronner, Stephen Eric, 1949-
A rumor about the Jews : antisemitism, conspiracy, and the
Protocols of Zion / Stephen Eric Bronner.
p. cm.
Includes bibliographical references and index.
ISBN 0-312-21804-4 (cloth) ISBN 0-19-516956-5 (pbk.)
1. Protocols of the wise men of Zion Juvenile literature.
2. Antisemitism Juvenile literature.
I. Title.
DS145.P7B76 2000
305.892'4—dc21   99-42576
                                                                 CIP

Design by planettheo.com

10 9 8 7 6 5 4 3 2 1

Printed in the United States of America

To the German Jews who,
forced into exile by the Nazis,
built a community and rebuilt their lives in
Washington Heights near the northern tip of Manhattan

CONTENTS

PREFACE TO THE PAPERBACK EDITION

A Rumor about the Jews provided a new critical way of thinking about anti-Semitism. It treated an enormously popular fabrication of a conspiracy by Jews to take over the world, *The Protocols of the Elders of Zion*, as part of a broader assault on the civilizing impulse and the liberal, secular, egalitarian heritage of the Enlightenment. My book was never intended as a history of anti-Semitism, contrary to some critics, but rather as a genealogy of its historical variants, a way of thinking about the significant differences within an anthropological prejudice, and an account of the existential reasons for its seductiveness. The book describes how this infamous forgery fashioned the Jew as the quintessential "other" of Christian civilization, how the self-absolving bigot sees himself, and the peculiar appeal of anti-Semitism to the "losers" in the struggle over modernity. With the precarious triumph of liberal democracy, I claimed, anti-Semitism had been pushed to the fringes of political life in the western democracies. But this was not meant to suggest that progress will somehow magically make prejudice disappear: only that a cosmopolitan, liberal and socialist, worldview is the most appropriate way of fighting it.

Cemetaries are still desecrated, attacks on Jews still occur, and the international community should pressure their governments for hate-crime legislation and treat bigotry against Jews like any other form of racism or discrimination. Anti-Semitism remains a latent threat and I noted not only that, ironically, "modernity invigorates the pre-modern" but that "the half-baked rumor might yet resurface as a full-blown myth with a new form of popular appeal."

The Protocols of Zion are, right now in these fraught times, making a come-back. Rumors abound that "the Jews" were responsible for 9/11 and the attack on the World Trade Center. There is the tiresomely familiar talk about the Jews controlling Wall Street and Hollywood. *The Matzah of Zion* published by Mustafa Tlas, the Syrian Minister of Defense, is now in its eighth edition: it offers an Arab version of the undying myth about how Jews use the blood of Christian children to bake their *matzah* for Passover. Most troubling of all, however, was the airing of a 41-part soap opera on Egyptian television, *Horse without a Horseman* (2002), which presented a history of the Middle East from 1855 through 1917. This work of sublime hatred celebrated the existence of a Jewish conspiracy, scenes of the "Elders of Zion" plotting their strategy, and the supposed discovery of *The Protocols of the Elders of Zion*. The old justification for employing the forgery was rolled out once again: it is not a pedantic matter of whether the tract is authentic since—according to what the star of the series, Muhammed Sobhi, told *The New York Times* (10/26/02)—"Zionism exists and it has controlled the world since the dawn of history."

Al-Jazeera aired some discussions critical of this project and, in general, such works require unequivocal denunciation by liberals and progressives within the Arab community. That is especially the case since the myth of a Jewish conspiracy has mostly been employed by right-wing Arab nationalists, especially the Ba'athists, in Iraq and Syria as well as by elements of the Muslim Brotherhood in Egypt. Official circles, in keeping with the past, use the *Protocols* when there is some semblance of popular discontent with the internal situation. Virtually no serious and independent Arab publications, however, have bothered with the *Protocols*. The matter of culpability has more to do with the silence of liberal voices than outright endorsement of the tract. In any event, having said all this, it is important to understand that the political priority for the Middle East is less anti-Semitism than the plight of those Arabs who suffer under Israeli rule.

This is—again—not to deny that anti-Semitism exists: only that it exists in a new and very different context: The Jews were once innocent victims of reactionary institutions and paranoid religious beliefs: they were fragmented and seen as unified, ostracized and seen as invasive, powerless and seen as omnipotent. The conspiratorial fears of Jewish world conquest lacked any trace of empirical justification and the anti-Semitic portrait of "the Jew" had nothing to do with living, breathing Jews. That, however, is no longer the case. Anti-Semitism, which was never an independent self-propelling impulse, has now become interwoven with the barbarous treatment of the Palestinians, the attempts to create a "greater Israel," and the policies of the United States in the Middle East. The Israeli state no less than advocacy organizations like the World Jewish Congress, the American Israel Public Affairs Committee, and the Anti-Defamation League, which trumpet every mention of the *Protocols* and consider every criticism of Israel tantamount to anti-Semitism, are producing their own version of "blowback." Their stance is fostering precisely the anti-Semitic attitudes that they wish to combat: less and less persuasive today is the attempt to invoke the memory of the holocaust in order to justify every reactionary twist and turn of Israeli policy.

Dealing with various anti-Semitic misperceptions like a plan for world conquest, in the first instance, is possible only by admitting that Jews are no longer in the ghetto or an oppressed minority. They now have a state and it is not some tiny, nearly defenseless, entity surrounded by bloodthirsty Arab savages. Israel is a nation with the seventh strongest military on the planet and the dominant power in the Middle East. It is the recipient of more than $4 billion in aid annually from the United States and it is the new darling of the Christian Coalition. Israeli settlements, populated primarily by fanatical Zionists and religious zealots, dot the West Bank and policies have been implemented akin to apartheid with respect to its own growing Arab citizenry. The Middle East provides a new context for anti-semitism and imbues it with a very different set of symbolic meanings than it had in Europe.

Anti-Semitism is no longer strongest where, according to Hannah Arendt, the Jew is visible without enjoying power or is "just visible enough." Israel is both visible and powerful and those who suffer from its brutal policies, increasingly desperate people driven by increasingly desperate circumstances, will grab at a scapegoat: anti-Semitism is now implicated in the response to a genuine crisis rather than merely an expression of simple paranoia, psychological projection, or existential legitimation.

To explain, however, is not to excuse: irrational prejudice and simple bigotry against Jews—as a people or a race—must now, more than ever, be disentangled from a critique of the Israeli state, its domestic politics, and its imperialist ambitions. Works like *Horse without a Horseman* undermine that effort. The vile attitudes they express only further poison the already polluted politics of the Middle East. They play into the hands of the worst elements in Israeli society thereby guaranteeing only a further downward spiral.

Anti-Semitism erodes the ability to distinguish between political groups and social interests within the Jewish community or the Israeli state: it is the reflection of a night in which all cows are black. Sound policy cannot be built on foolish assumptions. Anti-Semitism reinforces the dogmatic and unyielding division between "us" and "them." It thereby actually helps Jews avoid the need for choosing between a secular, democratic, and non-imperialist or a "Jewish," authoritarian, and imperialist state. Being reminded of the *Protocols*, envisioning a world of unchanging anti-Semitism, it is easy for them internalize the bigoted, a-historical, and paranoid thinking they should oppose.

Arab and Jewish fanatics have increasingly come to resemble one another in their xenophobia and self-righteousness, their intolerance and dogmatism, their contempt for cosmopolitanism and democracy. Trapped in the illusory world of the *Protocols*, they are complicit in revivifying an anachronistic prejudice. They remain the victims of that self-chosen blindness, so appealing and yet so dangerous, which originally served as the foil for *A Rumor about the Jews*.

ACKNOWLEDGMENTS

I would like to thank a number of friends and colleagues who made this a better book. Diana Judd provided invaluable help as my research assistant, and I appreciate greatly the comments on the manuscript offered by Anand Commissiong, John Ehrenberg, Irene Gendzier, Micheline Ishay, Kurt Jacobsen, Elizabeth Kelly, Manfred Steger, and Christian Fenner. Klaus-Pieter Schmidt and Hans-Ulrich Seebohm, my German translators, also provided important corrections and insights. As for my wife, Anne Burns, she again made all the difference.

Antisemitism is the rumor about the Jews.
—Theodor W. Adorno, *Minima Moralia*

ONE

Introduction

The *Protocols of the Elders of Zion* constitutes one of the most infamous documents of antisemitism. It consists of the supposed minutes from twenty-four sessions of a congress held by representatives from the "twelve tribes of Israel" and led by a Grand Rabbi, whose purpose was to plan the conquest of the world. This congress never took place. The pamphlet is actually a crude forgery created by the *Okhrana,* or secret police, of Imperial Russia. It first appeared in 1903 and it incorporates many of the most vicious myths about the Jews handed down over the centuries. Used initially to blame Jews and their supposedly servile allies, the Freemasons, for the 1905 Revolution in Russia, the *Protocols* would become a welcome export around the world. If not simple hatred then pogroms, and if not pogroms then even worse, followed in its wake. It was applauded by royalty, it was embraced by counterrevolutionaries, and the Nazis made it required reading. It still serves as a staple for numerous fundamentalist, conservative, neofascist, and antisemitic groups in the United States and throughout the world. Indeed, what the real *Communist Manifesto* was for marxism, the fictitious *Protocols* was for antisemitism.

It enabled antisemites to see their nemesis, the Jew, as both an intrinsic element of western civilization and its *other.* This anthropological view, in fact, provides the foundation for the theory articulated in the pamphlet. Beyond the myriad ways in which hatred of the Jew is expressed lies the continuity of prejudice. The *Protocols* solidifies the connection between the true believers in Christianity, those nineteenth-century reactionaries intent on combating the Enlightenment, and the fanatics of a seemingly antireligious and revolutionary Nazi movement desirous of establishing the primacy of a single race. Christian institutions and the first genuinely reactionary movements, no less than the Nazis, overwhelmingly aligned themselves against the modern ideas and values generated in the age of democratic revolution: secularism and science, rationalism and materialism, tolerance and equality, capitalism and socialism, liberalism and marxism. Antisemitism was never simply an independent impulse. It was always part of a broader project directed against the civilizing impulse of reason and the dominant forces of modernity. The way in which the *Protocols* contributed to that effort is what this book seeks to explore.

My personal background surely shaped my interest in the *Protocols:* my family fled Hitler's Germany and I grew up during the postwar period in a neighborhood of working-class German-Jewish immigrants who had experienced the implications of this terrible pamphlet in a way beyond my imagination. Those still alive continue to exist in the shadow of the holocaust. It remains their point of reference for any outbreak of genocide or antisemitism; my parents and their friends will still often exclaim: *genau wie beim Hitler.* Many younger people have also undoubtedly felt the sting of antisemitism in their personal lives and encountered credulous individuals who have mentioned the *Protocols.* But it is woefully misleading to draw parallels between antisemitism as it was practiced in the 1930s and its practice today. In the West, few know much about this once-popular pamphlet and even fewer have read it.

International sales of the pamphlet were astronomical during the 1920s and 1930s; Henri Rollin, the French scholar of antisemitism, called the *Protocols* the most widely distributed book in the world other than the Bible, and its distribution was accompanied by a mountain of secondary literature comprising well more than one thousand titles. Since World War II, however, antisemitism has receded and, on closer examination, the mountain has dwindled in size. The tract is no longer the fundamental ideological expression of an organized mass movement capable of influencing the politics of western nations. The world is different and it makes little sense to look at the present through the lenses of the past.

The *Protocols* is now almost universally recognized as a fabrication. Its claims about a Jewish world conspiracy are mostly greeted with derision in the western democracies. Despite all evidence to the contrary, of course, some still consider these calculatedly paranoiac myths true and the rumors plausible. Weakened forms of antisemitic politics still exist, and certain groups and movements are still susceptible to the message contained in the pamphlet. The danger of antisemitism never fully disappears and, in any event, the political risk in making the opposite assumption is too high. The half-baked rumor might yet resurface as a full-blown myth with a new form of popular appeal. The fragility of our historical memory alone justifies a new treatment of the *Protocols*. Nevertheless, if the issue is really one of preventing the recurrence of antisemitism, then it is less a matter of offering a pedantic account of the trials and tribulations associated with the *Protocols* than providing a sense of how it was shaped by certain historical trends and how it reflects them.

Just as there are documents of liberty like the *Declaration of Independence* (1776), or the *Gettysburg Address* (1863), there are also documents in which the face of hatred and tyranny appears. The *Protocols* is one of those works: it encapsulates the historical legacy of antisemitism and reflects its transformation from a religious and social concept into a new political phenomenon. The pamphlet gives an insight into the way the antisemite thinks, not merely about the Jew but about himself or herself. It also gives an ugly insight into the utterly ruthless and unscrupulous, if sometimes self-deceiving, assumptions of right-wing extremists— whether they are "sincerely" antisemitic or not. Indeed, if this tract exhibits the uniqueness of antisemitism, it also highlights the way in which this prejudice is grounded within an antimodern and antidemocratic worldview.

Generating these insights is possible only if the *Protocols* is seen not merely as an outrageous set of lies born of prejudice but as a seminal contribution within what was an established tradition of intellectual life intent on developing an explicitly antiliberal and antisocialist political project. The forgery was perpetrated in Imperial Russia. Yet virtually the same story could easily have unfolded elsewhere. Antisemitism was an international phenomenon and the *Protocols* is not simply reducible to the Russian context in which it was conceived. Important works—even fraudulent ones—take on a life of their own and that is clearly the case with this tract. The *Protocols* helped shape the mass movements, revolutions, and wars of the twentieth century. History is not merely composed of truth: it incorporates lies as well.

Other works are arguably more seminal for the intellectual lineage of antisemitism. But they generally run hundreds of pages, and they were mostly directed toward an educated or academic audience. Nor should this appear strange given the respectability accorded antisemitism in many cultivated circles prior to World War II. The *Protocols,* by contrast, fits nicely into a newspaper or a set of magazine installments. Even though one of its first appearances was in the form of an elegant gold-leaf edition meant for Czar Nicholas II, from the first, the tract was intended for a mass audience.

The *Protocols* is not a work of intellectual quality. It is short on ideas and shorter on argumentation. Its vision is gothic and a spirit of cheap melodrama permeates the tract. The writing is pathetic. Its convoluted prose, logical inconsistencies, and impoverished imagery betray the character and intellectual level of its authors. The brochure rests on traditional myths even as it gives a distinctly modern twist to the prejudices of the past: it, indeed, offers a sense of the fears raised by "the Jews."

The *Protocols* form the basis for these reflections on antisemitism. Given the general lack of acquaintance with this work of antisemitism for popular consumption, it is perhaps useful to provide some selections. The *Protocols* appeared in many formats. But, for present purposes, the popular English translation by Victor Marsden is the most appropriate. The selections included in the next chapter are more extensive than most, and they should provide a sense of what fascists themselves considered important about the pamphlet. They will also enable the reader to avoid dealing with a rambling and redundant work of nearly a hundred pages. The central idea of the *Protocols* involves the supposed Jewish world conspiracy designed to enslave Christian civilization under a new world order run by the leading elder of Zion. But there are other claims and various hidden assumptions. It is important to consider the imagery of the work, the stereotypes it employs, and the provincial anxieties it creates with respect to the supposed degeneration of the authentic community and its racially homogeneous inhabitants.

Antisemites were unconcerned with empirical reality, and their progressive critics must understand the assumptions informing their arguments. The *Protocols* portrays the Jews and Freemasons as outsiders and enemies of Christian civilization. It highlights their seemingly strange and outlandish rituals, their supposedly secret symbols and secret contacts. It condemns their influence, their control over media, and their manipulation of the most diverse political parties. It projects the antisemites' own authoritarianism upon them and, oddly enough, it admires the absolute obedience supposedly commanded by the Grand Rabbi or Grand Master. The Jew and the Freemason are one and the same or else the Jew is the master and the Freemason his lackey. It is the same nonsense packaged differently. "The Jew" has nothing to do with Jews.

The *Protocols* is expressive of an anthropological trend within the "Judeo-Christian" heritage, and the third chapter of this book, "The Text in Context," attempts to make sense of it. It provides a geneology and a sketch of what William James might have termed the "varieties of antisemitism" and the logic driving the historical development of this particular prejudice. It also provides a sense of the cultural atmosphere in which the tract came into existence and its opposition to the civilizing forces of secularism and modernity, justice and tolerance, individualism and democracy. The pamphlet is shown to mirror the feelings of powerlessness, the paranoia, and the fear of the losers who are content to see the "hidden hand" of the Jews pulling the strings of progress. This chapter indeed makes abundantly clear that the strengthening of prejudice is the other side of the struggle for liberty, equality, and fraternity.

The chapter begins with an examination of premodern religious bigotry in which Christians believed that Jews were working together with the devil: these believers were more concerned with abolishing the faith of the Jew than refusing to recognize him as a person. The situation changed in the aftermath of the Enlightenment and the age of democratic revolution when, fearful of Jews making use of their universal rights as individual citizens, reactionaries sought to retract the privileges Jews had gained and essentially to recreate the ghetto. This meant nothing less than implicitly recognizing the Jew as a Jew while refusing to consider him or her as a person capable of participating in the public realm. Only following the First World War would anti-semitic mass parties attempt to deny the Jew as an individual endowed with rights and as a Jew. This fateful development would serve as the ideological precondition of the holocaust.

With the stage set, "The Tale of a Forgery" recounts the story behind the fabrication of the *Protocols*. It underwent numerous permutations and various versions have been ascribed to various individuals. But there is no need to rehearse once again the numerous esoteric elements of the plot or to provide a literary comparison of the numerous editions in which the pamphlet appeared. The true drama lies in the creation of what would become the most popular edition of the *Protocols* and the purposes it was meant to serve. All of this presupposes a more critical look at the period extending roughly from the last decade of the nineteenth century until the outbreak of World War I. The period is commonly known as "the good years" or *la belle époque*. But such terms obscure the reality: Imperial Russia was beset by a profound economic, political, and spiritual crisis and, soon enough, its implications would be felt in Europe. The *Protocols* serve to illuminate the character of the crisis and the reactionary response to it.

"Spreading the News" explores the career of the forgery. It had originally inspired the pogroms organized by the infamous "Black Hundreds" in Imperial Russia. But this was only the beginning. The *Action Française,* the first mass-based reactionary movement, would make use of it in its struggle against progressive forces in the 1920s and the Popular Front in the 1930s. *Opus Dei,* itself a secretive elite given to conspiratorial views and practices, employed the *Protocols* to explain the Jewish peril to Catholics. The pamphlet inspired assassinations of political figures and its fame spread to Southern Europe and the Baltic.

Antisemites of every stripe took it to heart. There were the fanatics like Ludwig Müller, otherwise known as Müller von Hausen or Gottfried zur Beek, the editor of the German edition of the *Protocols,* and Alfred Rosenberg, the future philosopher of the Third Reich, who defended it. There were great industrialists like Henry Ford, who sponsored its American publication. There were important figures like Ezra Pound and Louis-Ferdinand Céline, artistic innovators and political fools, who embraced its central thesis. And there was also, of course, Hitler himself who sought to implement its practical implications.

Countless other politicians and intellectuals were either duped by the *Protocols* or made use of the pamphlet in a calculated fashion. But there were also those who fought against its pernicious influence. The battle against this antisemitic tract was indeed an important episode in the larger ideological and political battle against fascism. That is why it is also necessary to mention the efforts of figures like Pierre Charles, Lucien Wolf, Binjamin Segel, and Rev. Elias Newman to expose the pamphlet as a fraud, and the sensational Swiss trial of the 1930s in which the Nazis were forced to substantiate their belief in its authenticity.

The trial should have settled matters. But it didn't. Or, at least, not completely. The *Protocols* became the tool of new movements: fascists looking back at the past, neofascists dreaming of the future, national movements seeking to employ antisemitism for their ideological ends. But the tract reemerged in a new context: the holocaust created a new revulsion for antisemitism, Israel was constructed as an island of safety for Jews, and new organizations in most western nations arose to combat the old myths and the old hatreds. The political salience of antisemitism has changed and the *Protocols* is no more a living document than *Mein Kampf.* It currently plays an auxiliary role in movements far less threatening than those of the 1920s. Nevertheless, if political antisemitism is now mostly latent, it might still resurface and take dangerous forms.

Antisemitism need not always remain in cold storage: its anachronistic quality can prove attractive for supporters looking back to
the "good old days." Its appeal clearly derives from its ability to
present itself as a philosophy from the gut, fueled by resentment and
despair. Antisemitism highlights the irrational, the stereotypical, and
the intuitive. It provides a form of self-justification and compensa-
tion for the *losers* or those who have lost faith in progress. This
prejudice reinforces the connection between their ideas, their interests, and their understanding of history. "The Legacy of a Lie," the
conclusion to this volume, uses the *Protocols* to illuminate the status
of contemporary antisemitism and the unique world of prejudice and
paranoia inhabited by the antisemite.

Hatred of the Jew is a lived experience. Antisemitism responds
not merely to economic or political needs but to existential needs
as well. There is clearly a difference between the insincere utilizers
of antisemitic prejudice and its sincere, if gullible, consumers. But
simply disproving the various falsehoods of works like the *Protocols*
is insufficient. Antisemitism is ultimately, in practical political
terms, a matter of *faith:* arguments become legitimate only insofar
as they support the claim made on faith. Antisemitism *presupposes*
a belief in the overwhelming power of an evil Jew. The *Protocols*
casts a special light on it: the fanatical antisemite turns the Jew into
more than the scapegoat. The Jew is responsible because the
antisemite is not. The omnipotence of the Jew, in short, reflects the
impotence of the antisemite.

The Jew apparently achieved such overwhelming power
because the Jew is a *chameleon* capable of taking different forms at
different times: the Jew *is* not the homosexual supposedly bringing
about the moral decay of society, or the capitalist supposedly
consumed by private greed, or the communist supposedly intent
upon overthrowing "civilization." The *Protocols* makes clear that
the Jew is all of the above and more: the chameleon can assume the
form of *any* enemy required by any particular victim. The Jew
opposes the populace at every turn: the historical connection
between populism and antisemitism is no accident. The *chameleon-
effect* explains the ability of the Jew to manipulate international

events; it shows why the Christian is always outwitted and why, in the mind of the fanatic, both the Jew and the need for antisemitism have persisted in various forms from the very beginnings of Judeo-Christian civilization.

The *Protocols* provides a mirror image of history: the powerless become all powerful and the all powerful become powerless. The pamphlet turns truth on its head. But the truth doesn't disappear. Indeed, for precisely this reason, the critic must uncover what the lie denies: the task is to show how this brochure, even as it attempts to legitimate the repression of a seemingly all-powerful enemy, actually illuminates the opprobrium borne by a powerless group of people. The forgery demonstrates the dangerous political trajectory of antimodernist or anti-Enlightenment thinking. It offers an insight into the perverse and self-serving ways in which Christians have seen Jews for most of western history. It portrays the stereotypes and the Manichean elements within Christian dogma. It shatters the comfortable illusion of a Judeo-Christian heritage.

All western and many other states have their traditions of antisemitism. It is difficult to gauge where the ideology was "worst." The translation of the antisemitic word into the antisemitic deed depended primarily upon political factors. Little wonder then that the most favored lands for Jewish immigration should have been those with the most liberal political institutions. Liberal political institutions and a democratic public sphere may not always prove victorious against their intolerant and authoritarian enemies. But the truism holds: institutions genuinely grounded in civic republicanism and cosmopolitan attitudes are the best guarantees against antisemitism or racism of any sort. Jews have historically stood in the forefront of those demanding the creation of such institutions and the hegemony of such values. It remains perhaps the best part of the Jewish political tradition; it is also surely becoming among the most undervalued as parochial forms of nationalist extremism and religious fundamentalism greet the introduction of the twenty-first century.

Integral nationalism and messianic visions of a Christian destiny have always intoxicated antisemites. But these same values are currently embraced by an increasing number of Jews themselves.

They worry over the erosion of their religion and identity. They resent the trend towards religious pluralism and the introduction of cosmopolitan values into their community. They show only contempt for liberal democracy though, ironically, its institutions remain the best guarantees against the exercise of arbitrary power and the force of prejudice. The victims of antisemitism are not immune from the thinking of their persecutors. Jews, too, can unwittingly succumb to the *Protocols*. No less than illuminating the tradition of antisemitism and evaluating its contemporary status, exposing this danger is among the most important aims of *A Rumor about the Jews*.

Antisemitism for Popular Consumption: Selections from The *Protocols of the Elders of Zion* [1]

INTRODUCTION BY VICTOR MARSDEN (1922)

These Protocols give the substance of addresses delivered to the innermost circle of the Rulers of Zion . . . Parts and summaries of the plan have been published from time to time during the centuries as the secrets of the Elders have leaked out . . . It demonstrates that the Jews are now a world menace and that the Aryan races will have to domicile them permanently out of Europe. Who are the Elders? This is a secret which has not been revealed. They are the Hidden Hand.

PROTOCOL 1

[A.] What I am about to set forth, then, is our system from the two points of view, that of ourselves and that of the *goyim,* i.e. non-Jews . . .

[B.] Our power in the present tottering conditions of all forms of power will be more invincible than any other, because it will remain invisible until the moment when it has gained such strength that no cunning can any longer undermine it . . .

[C.] Let us, however, in our plans, direct our attention not so much to what is good and moral as to what is necessary and useful . . .

[D.] We must not stop at bribery, deceit and treachery when they should serve toward the attainment of our end . . .

[E.] Far back in ancient times we were the first to cry among the masses of the people the words "Liberty, Equality, Fraternity" . . . [These words] brought to our ranks, thanks to our blind agents, whole legions who bore our banners with enthusiasm. And all the time these words were cankerworms at work boring into the well-being of the *goyim*, and putting an end everywhere to peace, quiet, solidarity, and destroying all the foundations of the *goya* states. As you will see later, this helped us to our triumph; it gave us the possibility among other things of getting into our hands the master card—the destruction of the privileges, or in other words of the very existence of the aristocracy of the *goyim*, that class which was the only defence peoples and countries had against us. On the ruins of the natural and genealogical aristocracy of the *goyim* we have set up the aristocracy of our educated class headed by the aristocracy of money. The qualifications for this aristocracy we have established in wealth, which is dependent upon us, and in knowledge, for which our learned elders provide the motive force.

PROTOCOL 2

[A.] It is indispensable, for our purpose that wars, so far as possible, should not result in territorial gains; war will thus be brought onto the economic ground, where the nations will not fail to perceive in the assistance we give the strength of our predominance and this state of things will put both sides at the mercy of our international *agentur;* which possesses millions of eyes ever on the watch and unhampered by any limitations whatsoever? Our international rights will then wipe out national rights, in the proper sense of right, and will rule the nations precisely as the civil law of States rule the relations of their subjects among themselves.

[B.] . . . The intellectuals of the *goyim* will puff themselves up with their knowledge and without any logical verification of them will put into effect all the information available from science, which our *agentur* specialists have cunningly pieced together for the purpose of educating their minds in the direction we want. Do not suppose for a moment that these statements are empty words: think carefully of the successes we arranged for Darwinism, Marxism, Nietzsche-ism. To us Jews, at any rate, it should be plain to see what a disintegrating importance these directives have had upon the minds of the *goyim* . . .

[C.] It is in the Press that the triumph of freedom of speech finds its incarnation. But the *goyim* States have not known how to make use of this force; and it has fallen into our hands. Through the Press we have gained the power to influence while remaining ourselves in the shade; thanks to the Press we have got the *gold* in our hands, notwithstanding that we have had to gather it out of oceans of blood and tears.

PROTOCOL 3

[A.] Today I may tell you that our goal is now only a few steps off. There remains a small space to cross and the whole long path we have trodden is ready now to close its cycle of the Symbolic Snake by which we symbolize our people. When this ring closes, all the States of Europe will be locked in its coil as in a powerful vise . . .

[B.] In order to incite seekers after power to a misuse of power we have set all forces in opposition one to another . . . The people under our guidance have annihilated the aristocracy who were their one and only defence and foster-mother for the sake of their own advantage which is inseparably bound up with the well-being of the people. Nowadays, with the destruction of the aristocracy, the people have fallen into the grips of merciless money-grinding scoundrels who have laid a pitiless and cruel yoke upon the necks of the workers. We appear on the scene as alleged saviors of the worker from this oppression when we propose to him to enter the ranks of our fighting forces— Socialists, Anarchists, Communists—to whom we always give support in accordance with an alleged brotherly rule (of the solidarity of all humanity) of our *social masonry*. The aristocracy, which enjoyed by law the labour of the workers, was interested in seeing that the workers were well fed, healthy and strong. We are interested in just the opposite—in the diminution, the *killing out of the goyim* . . .

[C.] This hatred will be still further magnified by the effects of an *economic crisis*, which will stop dealings on the exchanges and bring industry to a standstill. We shall create by all the secret subterranean methods open to us and with the aid of gold, which is all in our hands, *a universal economic crisis whereby we shall throw upon the streets whole mobs of workers simultaneously in all the countries of Europe* . . .

[D.] Remember the French Revolution, to which it was we who gave the name of *Great:* the secrets of its preparation are well known to us for it was wholly the work of our hands. Ever since that time we have been leading the peoples from one disenchantment to another, so that in the end they should turn also from us in favour of that *King Despot of the blood of Zion, whom we are preparing for the world.*

PROTOCOL 4

[A.] *Gentile* masonry, blindly serves as a screen for us and our objects, but the plan of action of our force, even its very abiding place, remains for the whole people an unknown mystery . . .

[B.] But even freedom might be harmless and have its place in the State economy without injury to the well-being of the peoples if it rested upon the foundation of faith in God, upon the brotherhood of humanity, unconnected with the conception of equality, which is negative by the very laws of creation, for they have established subordination. With such a faith as this a people might be governed by a wardship of parishes and would walk contentedly and humbly under the guiding hand of its spiritual pastor submitting to the dispositions of God on earth. This is the reason: why it is *indispensable for us to undermine all faith, to tear out of the minds of the* GOYIM *the very principle of the Godhead, and the spirit, and to put in its place arithmetical calculations and material needs.* In order to give the *goyim* no time to think and take note, their minds must be diverted towards industry and trade. Thus, all the nations will be swallowed up in the pursuit of gain and in the race for it will not take note of their common foe.

PROTOCOL 5

[A.] In the times when peoples looked upon kings on their thrones as on a pure manifestation of the will of God, they submitted without a murmur to the despotic power of kings; but from the day when we insinuated into their minds the conception of their own rights they began to regard the occupants of the thrones as mere ordinary mortals. The holy unction of the Lord's Anointed has fallen from the heads of kings in the eye of the people, and when we also robbed them of their faith in God the might of power was flung upon the streets into the place of public proprietorship and was seized by us . . .

[B.] Reared on analysis, observation, on delicacies of fine calculation, in this species of skill we have no rivals, any more than we have either in the drawing up of plans of political actions and solidarity. In this respect the Jesuits alone might have compared with us, but we have contrived to discredit them in the eyes of the unthinking mob as an overt organization, while we ourselves all the while have kept our secret organization in the shade. However, it is probably all the same to the world who is its sovereign lord, whether the head of Catholicism or our despot of the blood of Zion! But to us, the Chosen People, it is very far from being a matter of indifference . . .

[C.] *The nations cannot come to even an inconsiderable private agreement without our secretly having a hand in it* . . . All the wheels of the machinery of all States go by the force of the engine, which is in our hands, and that engine of the machinery of States is—Gold. The science of political economy invented by our learned elders has for long past been giving royal prestige to capital . . .

[D.] *The principal object of our directorate consists in this: to debilitate the public mind by criticism . . . In order to put the public opinion into our hands we must bring it into a state of bewilderment by giving expression from all sides to so many contradictory opinions and for such length of time as will suffice to make the* GOYIM *lose their heads and come to see that the best thing is to have no opinion of any kind in matters political,* which is not given to the public to understand, because they are understood only by him who guides the public. This is the first secret. The second secret requisite for the success of our government is comprised in the following: to multiply to such an extent national failings, habits, passions, conditions of civil life, that it will be impossible for anyone to know where he is in the resulting chaos, so that the people in consequence will fail to understand one another. This measure will also serve us in another way, namely, to sow discord in all parties, to dislocate all collective forces, which are still unwilling to submit to us, and to discourage any kind of personal initiative which might in any degree hinder our affair. *There is nothing more dangerous than personal initiative;* if it has genius behind it, such initiative can do more than can be done by millions of people among whom we have sown discord . . .

[E.] *By all these means we shall so wear down the* GOYIM *they will be compelled to offer us international power of a nature that by its position will enable us without any violence gradually to absorb all the State forces of the world and to form a* Super-Government. In place of the rulers of today we shall set up a bogey which will be called the Super-Government administration. Its hands will reach out in all directions like nippers and its organization will be of such colossal dimensions that it cannot fail to subdue all the nations of the world.

PROTOCOL 6

[A.] We shall soon begin to establish huge monopolies, reservoirs of colossal riches upon which even large fortunes of the *goyim* will depend to such an extent that they will go to the bottom together with the credit of the states on the day after the political smash . . .

[B.] The aristocracy of the *goyim* as a political force is dead—we need not take it into account; but as landed proprietors they can still be harmful to us from the fact that they are self-sufficing in the resources upon which they live. It is essential therefore for us at whatever cost to deprive them of their land. This object will be best attained by increasing the burdens upon landed property—in loading lands with debts . . . What we want is that industry should drain off from the land both labour and capital and by means of speculation transfer into our hands all the money of the world, and thereby throw all the *goyim* into the ranks of the proletariat. Then the *goyim* will bow down before us, if for no other reason but to get the right to exist . . .

[C.] *We shall further undermine artfully and deeply sources of production by accustoming the workers to anarchy and to drunkenness and side by side therewith taking all measure to extirpate from the face of the earth all the educated forces of the* GOYIM.

PROTOCOL 7

[A.] Throughout all Europe, and by means of relations with Europe, in other continents also, we must create ferments, discords, and hostility . . . [B]y our intrigues we shall tangle up all the threads which we have stretched into the cabinets of all states by means of the political, by economic treaties, or loan obligations . . .

[B.] The principal factor of success in the political is the secrecy of its undertakings . . . We must compel the governments of the *goyim* to take action in the direction favored by our widely conceived plan, already approaching the desired consummation, by what we shall represent as public opinion, secretly prompted by us through the means of that so-called "Great Power"—*the Press, which, with a few exceptions that may be disregarded, is already entirely in our hands.*

PROTOCOL 8

[A.] Our directorate must surround itself with all these forces of civilization among which it will have to work. It will surround itself with publicists, practical jurists, administrators, diplomats and, finally, with persons prepared by a special super-educational training *in our special schools* . . .

[B.] Around us again will be a whole constellation of bankers, industrialists, capitalists and—*the main thing*— *millionaires—because in substance everything will be settled by the question of figures.* For a time, until there will no longer be any risk in entrusting responsible posts in our states to our brother-Jews, we shall put them in the hands of persons whose past and reputation are such that between them and the people lies an abyss, persons who in case of disobedience to our instructions, must face criminal charges or disappear—this in order to make them defend our interests to their last gasp.

PROTOCOL 9

[A.] *De facto* we have already wiped out every kind of rule except our own . . . Nowadays, if any States raise a protest against us, it is only *pro forma* at our discretion and by our direction, *for their anti-Semitism is indispensable to us for the management of our lesser brethren.*

[B.] And the weapons in our hands are limitless ambitions, burning greediness, merciless vengeance, hatreds and malice. It is from us that the all-engulfing terror proceeds. We have in our service persons of all opinions, of all doctrines, monarchists, demagogues, socialists, communists, and utopian dreamers of every kind. We have harnessed them all to the task: each one of them on his own account is boring away at the last remnants of authority, is striving to overthrow all established forms of order. By these acts, all states are in torture: they exhort to tranquility, are ready to sacrifice everything for peace: but we will not give them peace until they openly acknowledge our international Super-government, and with submissiveness.

[C.] Division into fractional parties has given them into our hands, for in order to carry on a contested struggle one must have money, and the money is all in our hands.

[D.] We have got our hands into the administration of the law, into the conduct of elections, into the press, into the liberty of the person, but principally into education and training as being the cornerstones of a free existence. We have fooled, bemused and corrupted the youth of the goyim by rearing them in principles and theories which are known to us to be false although it is by us that they have been inculcated.

PROTOCOL 10

[A.] . . . *We must have everybody vote without distinction of classes and qualifications,* in order to establish an absolute majority, which cannot be got from the educated propertied classes . . . When we introduced into the State organism the poison of Liberalism, its whole political complexion underwent a change. States have been seized with a mortal illness—blood poisoning. All that remains is to await the end of their death agony. Liberalism produced Constitutional States, which took the place of what was the only safeguard of the *goyim,* namely, Despotism; and *a constitution, as you well know, is nothing else but a school of discords,* misunderstandings, quarrels, disagreements, fruitless party agitations, party whims—in a word, a school of everything that serves to destroy the personality of State activity.

[B.] . . . We shall arrange elections in favor of such presidents as have in their past some dark, undiscovered stain, some "Panama" or other—then they will be trustworthy agents for the accomplishment of our plans out of fear of revelations and from the natural desire of everyone who has attained power, namely, the retention of the privileges, advantages, and honor connected with the office of president. The chamber of deputies will provide cover for, will protect, will elect, presidents, but we shall take from it the right to propose new, or make changes in existing laws, for this right will be given by us to the responsible president, a puppet in our hands.

[C.] But you yourselves perfectly well know that *to produce the possibility of the expression of such wishes by all the nations it is indispensable to trouble in all countries the people's relations with their governments so as to utterly exhaust humanity with dissension, hatred, struggle, envy and even by the use of torture, by starvation BY THE INOCULATION OF DISEASES, by want, so that the GOYIM see no other issue than to take refuge in our complete sovereignty in money and in all else. But if we give the nations of the world a breathing space the moment we long for is hardly likely ever to arrive.*

PROTOCOL 11

[A.] Having established approximately the *modus agendi* we will occupy ourselves with details of those combinations by which we have still to complete the revolution in the course of the machinery of State in the direction already indicated. By these combinations I mean the freedom of the Press, the right of association, freedom of conscience, the voting

principle, and many another that must disappear forever
from the memory of man . . .

[B.] The *goyim* are a flock of sheep, and we are their
wolves. And you know what happens when the wolves get
hold of the flock? . . .

[C.] For what purpose then have we invented this whole
policy and insinuated it into the minds of the *goys* without
giving them any chance to examine its underlying meaning? For what indeed if not in order to obtain in a
roundabout way what is for our scattered tribe unattain-
able by the direct road? It is this which has served as the
basis for our organization of SECRET MASONRY
WHICH IS NOT KNOWN TO, AND AIMS WHICH
ARE NOT EVEN SO MUCH AS SUSPECTED BY,
THESE GOY CATTLE, ATTRACTED BY US INTO
THE "SHOW" ARMY OF MASONIC LODGES IN
ORDER TO THROW DUST IN THE EYES OF
THEIR FELLOWS.

[D.] God has granted to us, His Chosen People, the gift of
the dispersion, and in this which appears in all eyes to be
our weakness, has come forth all our strength, which has
now brought us to the threshold of sovereignty over all the
world.

PROTOCOL 12

[A.] What is the part played by the press today? It serves
to excite and inflame those passions which are needed for
our purpose or else it serves selfish ends of parties. It is
often vapid, unjust, mendacious, and the majority of the
public have not the slightest idea what ends the press really
serves. We shall saddle and bridle it with a tight curb; we

shall do the same also with all productions of the printing press, for where would be the sense of getting rid of the attacks of the press if we remain targets for pamphlets and books?

[B.] . . . *I beg you to note that among those making attacks upon us will also be organs established by us, but they will attack exclusively points that we have predetermined to alter. Not a single announcement will reach the public without our control.*

[C.] Is there any one of us who does not know that these phantom blessings are the direct roads to foolish imaginings which give birth to anarchical relations of men among themselves and towards authority, because progress, or rather the idea of progress, has introduced the conception of every kind of emancipation, but has failed to establish its limits . . . All the so-called liberals are anarchists, if not in fact, at any rate in thought. Every one of them is hunting after phantoms of freedom, and falling exclusively into license, that is into the anarchy of protest for the sake of protest . . .

[D.] All our newspapers will be of all possible complexions—aristocratic, republican, revolutionary, even anarchical . . . Like the Indian idol Vishnu they will have a hundred hands, and every one of them will have a finger on any one of the public opinions as required. When a pulse quickens, these hands will lead opinion in the direction of our aims, for an excited patient loses all power of judgment and easily yields to suggestions. Those fools who will think they are repeating the opinion of a newspaper of their own camp will be repeating our opinion or any opinion that seems desirable for us. In the vain belief that they are following the orders of their party they will in fact follow the flag which we hang out for them.

PROTOCOL 13

[A.] The need for daily bread forces the *goyim* to keep silence and be our humble servants . . .

[B.] In order that the masses themselves may not guess what we are about we further distract them with amusements, games, pastimes, passions, people's palaces . . . these interests will finally distract their minds from questions in which we should find ourselves compelled to oppose them.

[C.] . . . Have we not with complete success turned the brainless heads of the goyim with progress, till there is not among the goyim one mind able to perceive that under this word lies a departure from truth in all cases where it is not a question of material inventions, for truth is one and in it there is no place for progress. Progress, like a fallacious idea, serves to obscure truth so that none may know it except us, the Chosen of God, its guardians.

[D.] When we come into our kingdom, our orators will expound great problems which have turned humanity upside down in order to bring it at the end under our beneficent rule. Who will ever suspect then that ALL THESE PEOPLES WERE STAGE-MANAGED BY US ACCORDING TO A POLITICAL PLAN WHICH NO ONE HAS SO MUCH AS GUESSED AT IN THE COURSE OF MANY CENTURIES.

PROTOCOL 14

[A.] When we come into our kingdom, it will be undesirable for us that there should exist any other religion than ours of the One God with whom our destiny is bound up by our position as the Chosen People and through whom our same destiny is united with the destinies of the world. We must therefore sweep away all other forms of belief . . .

[B.] Our philosophers will discuss all the shortcomings of the various beliefs of the *goyim*. BUT NO ONE WILL EVER BRING UNDER DISCUSSION OUR FAITH FROM ITS TRUE POINT OF VIEW SINCE THIS WILL BE FULLY LEARNED BY NONE SAVE OURS, WHO WILL NEVER DARE TO BETRAY ITS SECRETS.

PROTOCOL 15

[A.] The principal guarantee of stability of rule is to confirm the aureole of power, and this aureole is attained only by such a majestic inflexibility of might as shall carry on its face the emblems of inviolability from mystical causes — from the choice of God. *Such was, until recent times, the Russian autocracy, the one and only serious foe we had in the world, without counting the Papacy.*

[B.] . . . We shall create and multiply free Masonic lodges in all the countries of the world, absorb into them all who may become or who are prominent in public activity, for in these lodges we shall find our principal intelligence office and means of influence. All these lodges we shall bring under one central administration, known to us alone and to all others absolutely unknown, which will be composed of our learned elders. The lodges will have their representatives who will serve to screen the above-mentioned administration of *masonry* and from whom will issue the watchword and programme. In these lodges we shall tie together the knot which binds together all revolutionary and liberal elements . . .

[C.] . . . Death is the inevitable end for all. It is better to bring that end nearer to those who hinder our affairs than to ourselves, to the founders of this affair. *We execute masons in such wise that none save the brotherhood can ever have a suspicion of it, not even the victims themselves of our death sentence, they all die when required as if from a normal kind of illness* . . . Knowing this, even the brotherhood in its turn dare not protest. By such methods we have plucked out of the midst of masonry the very root of protest against our disposition. While preaching liberalism to the *goyim* we at the same time keep our own people and our agents in a state of unquestioning submission . . .

[D.] . . . When the King of Israel sets upon his sacred head the crown offered him by Europe he will become patriarch of the world. The indispensable victims offered by him in consequence of their suitability will never reach the number of victims offered in the course of centuries by the mania of magnificence, the emulation between the *goy* governments.

PROTOCOL 16

[A.] In order to effect the destruction of all collective forces except ours we shall emasculate the first stage of collectivism—*the universities* by re-educating them in a new direction. *Their officials and professors will be prepared for their business by detailed secret programmes of action from which they will not with immunity diverge, not by one iota. They will be appointed with especial precaution and will be so placed as to be wholly dependent upon the Government.*

[B.] We must introduce into [gentile] education all those principles which have so brilliantly broken up their order. But when we are in power we shall remove every kind of disturbing subject from the course of education and shall make out of the youth obedient children of authority, loving him who rules as the support and hope of peace and quiet.

[C.] . . . *The occasional genius has always managed and always will manage to slip through into other states of life, but it is the most perfect folly for the sake of this rare occasional genius to let through into ranks foreign to them the untalented who thus rob of their places those who belong to those ranks by birth or employment. You know yourselves in what all this has ended for the goyim who allowed this crying absurdity.*

PROTOCOL 17

[A.] . . . *We have long past taken care to discredit the priesthood of the goyim* and thereby to ruin their mission on earth which in these days might still be a great hindrance to us. Day by day its influence on the peoples of the world is falling lower. *Freedom of conscience* has been declared everywhere, *so that now only years divide us from the moment of the complete wrecking of that Christian religion:* as to other religions we shall have still less difficulty in dealing with them, but it would be premature to speak of this now. We shall set clericalism and clericals into such narrow frames as to make their influence move in retrogressive proportion to its former progress.

[B.] *Just as nowadays our brethren are obliged at their own risk to denounce to the kabal apostates of their own family* or members who have been noticed doing anything in opposition to the *kabal, so in our kingdom over all the world it will be obligatory for all our subjects to observe the duty of service to the State in this direction.*

PROTOCOL 18

[A.] . . . It must be remembered that the prestige of authority is lessened if it frequently discovers conspiracies against itself: this implies a presumption of consciousness of weakness, or what is still worse, of injustice. You are aware that we have broken the prestige of the *goy* kings by frequent attempts upon their lives through our agents, blind sheep of our flock, who are easily moved by a few liberal phrases to crimes provided only they be painted in political colors. *We have compelled the rulers to acknowledge their weakness in advertising overt measures of secret defence and thereby we shall bring the promise of authority or destruction.*

PROTOCOL 19

We have done our best, and I hope we have succeeded to obtain that the *goyim* should not arrive at this means of contending with sedition. It was for this reason that through the Press and in speeches, indirectly — in cleverly compiled schoolbooks on history, we have advertised the martyrdom alleged to have been accepted by sedition-mongers for the idea of the commonweal. This advertisement has increased the contingent of liberals and has brought thousands of *goyim* into the ranks of our livestock cattle.

PROTOCOL 20

[A.] Today we shall touch upon the financial programme, which I put off to the end of my report as being the most difficult, the crowning and the decisive point of our plans . . . Taxation will best be covered by a progressive tax on property . . . State needs must be paid by those who will not feel the burden and have enough to take from . . . Purchase, receipt of money or inheritance will be subject to payment of a stamp progressive tax . . .

[B.] From these sums will be organized public works. The initiative in works of this kind, proceeding from State sources, will bind the working class firmly to the interests of the State and to those who reign.

[C.] Economic crises have been produced by us for the *goyim* by no other means than the withdrawal of money from circulation. Huge capitals have stagnated, withdrawing money from States, which were constantly obliged to apply to those same stagnant capitals for loans. These loans burdened the finances of the State with the payment of interest and made them the bond slaves of these capitals . . . The concentration of industry in the hands of capitalists out of the hands of small masters has drained away all the juices of the peoples and with them also of the States.

[D.] *You are aware that the gold standard has been the ruin of the States which adopted it, for it has not been able to satisfy the demands for money, the more so that we have removed gold from circulation as far as possible.*

[E.] With us the standard that must be introduced is the cost of working-man power, whether it be reckoned in paper or in wood. We shall make the issue of money in accordance with the normal requirements of each subject, adding to the quantity with every birth and subtracting with every death.

PROTOCOL 21

We shall replace the money markets by grandiose government credit institutions, the object of which will be to fix the price of industrial values in accordance with government views. These institutions will be in a position to fling upon the market five hundred millions of industrial paper in one day, or to buy up for the same amount. In this way all industrial undertakings will come into dependence upon us.

PROTOCOL 22

In our hands is the greatest power of our day—gold: in two days we can procure from our storehouses any quantity we may please. Surely there is no need to seek further proof that our rule is predestined by God? Surely we shall not fail with such wealth to prove that all that evil which for so many centuries we have had to commit has served at the end of ends the cause of true well being—the bringing of everything into order?

PROTOCOL 23

The supreme lord who will replace all now existing rulers, dragging on their existence among societies demoralized by us, societies that have denied even the authority of God, from whose midst breaks out on all sides the fire of anarchy, must first of all proceed to quench this all-devouring name. Therefore he will be obliged to kill off those existing societies, though he should drench them with his own blood, that he may resurrect them again in the form of regularly organized troops fighting con-sciously with every kind of infection that may cover the body of the State with sores. This chosen One of God is chosen from above to demolish the senseless forces moved by instinct and not reason, by brutishness and not humanness. These forces now triumph in manifestations of robbery and every kind of violence under the mask of principles of freedom and rights. They have overthrown all forms of social order to erect on the ruins the throne of the King of the Jews; but their part will be played out the moment he enters into his kingdom. Then it will be necessary to sweep them away from his path, on which must be left no knot, no splinter.

PROTOCOL 24

I pass now to the method of confirming the dynastic roots of King David to the last strata of the earth . . . Certain members of the seed of David will prepare the kings and their heirs, selecting not by right of heritage but by eminent capacities, inducting them into the most secret mysteries of the political, into schemes of government, but providing always that none may come to knowledge of the secrets. The object of this mode of action is that all may know that government cannot be entrusted to those who have not been inducted into the secret places of its art. To those persons only will be taught the practical application of the aforenamed plans . . . all the observations on the politico-economic moves and social sciences — in a word, all the spirit of laws which have been unshakably established by nature herself for the regulation of the relations of humanity.

THREE

The Text in Context:
The *Protocols* and the Varieties of Antisemitism[1]

For what a man had rather were true he more readily believes. Therefore he rejects difficult things from impatience of research; sober things, because they narrow hope; the deeper things of nature, from superstition; the light of experience, from arrogance and pride; things not commonly believed, out of deference to the opinion of the vulgar. Numberless in short are the ways, and sometimes imperceptible, in which the affections color and affect the understanding.

—Francis Bacon, *The New Organon* (1620)

Hatred of the Jew, or Judeophobia, was an inherent element of western civilization almost from its inception. Whatever the positive chapters in the history of Jewish-Christian relations, and they were relatively few prior to the Enlightenment of the eighteenth century, nowhere did Jews have genuine control over their fate or genuinely intermingle with gentile society as equals: their existence, for better or worse, overwhelmingly depended upon the whims of gentile rulers and alien institutions. If only for this reason, for the most part, Jews probably had as little use for their religious rivals as their rivals had for them. It would consequently be foolish to turn every critical utterance about Jews into an example of antisemitism and it would prove equally foolish to ignore the existence of real group conflicts in the formation of antisemitic ideology. Any serious inquiry into Judeophobia must subsequently highlight its qualitatively different religious, social, and political expressions.

Antisemitism is a phenomenon with several concentric levels or layers and economic jealousy is, arguably, only the most superficial of them.[2] Jews were initially the subject of primarily *religious intolerance:* they were despised for the arrogance of their monotheism, vilified as Christ's murderers, and identified with the devil. Later during the eighteenth and most of the nineteenth century, with the rise of capitalism, they would experience a *social* form of prejudice often termed *rishes.* It is a Yiddish word meaning malice that connotes a mixture of resentment and jealousy over the seeming ability of Jews to make good on the opportunities offered them by capitalism and liberal society. Only in the late nineteenth and early twentieth century, amid the cataclysmic developments associated with the triumph of modern life, would Jews experience the new *political* expression of Judeophobia commonly known as *antisemitism.* Only then would they would they find themselves popularly identified as a race, feared as an international threat to Christian civilization, and finally subjected to systematic genocide.

Antisemitism gives Judeophobia its programmatic form and distinctly modern character: it offers new ways of explaining history, provides new justifications for its prejudices, and begs the need for an all-encompassing political solution to the "Jewish question." The *Protocols of the Elders of Zion* reflects in theory the practical transition of a primarily religious prejudice that later became a social sentiment into a new political worldview. Religious intolerance of the Jews, *rishes,* and antisemitism always exist concurrently. Of interest is the particular mix among them. Political considerations surely had their impact upon the outbreak of religious intolerance in ancient Rome and the Middle Ages. *Rishes* was, moreover, clearly strengthened by religious prejudices.

And the modern form of political antisemitism made use of its predecessors: Nazi posters used to proclaim, for example, "He who knows the Jew knows the Devil."

Religious antisemitism is not simply superseded by social antisemitism, which then gives way to political antisemitism in some new variant of the historical stage theory employed by Hegel and Marx. Social occupations remained closed to Jews and inquisitions were also organized for political purposes during the Middle Ages when a religious form of antisemitism was obviously dominant. The basic point is simple: different mixtures of these antisemitic forms assume primacy at different historical moments. The unique role of the Jew not merely as a scapegoat but as the "other" of the non-Jew has, in short, taken different forms.

It is important to understand, however, that the hatred engendered by religious intolerance or by *rishes* is necessarily neither stronger nor weaker than that produced by political antisemitism. Each has its existential attraction and explanatory power. Each is rooted in historical images of Jews and Jewish life. Each is functional within a particular form of social organization. Each contributed in its own way to what would become an eliminationist or a redemptive solution to the problem of the Jews. Each connects a certain set of ideals with self-interested motives. Each mixes principle and opportunism in a manner foreign to other ideologies.

The varieties of Judeophobia blend with one another in practice: it is often difficult to distinguish where religious intolerance ends and *rishes* or antisemitism begins. This makes it all the more important to determine which was predominant in what historical setting and the ways in which the configuration of Judeophobia changed over time. Different configurations of antisemitism, after all, obviously have had different implications for its victims. Only when this is taken into account is it possible to understand the importance of the *Protocols* or the manner in which this idiotic pamphlet, variants of which supposedly had been discovered from time to time over the centuries, could employ earlier myths and transform them into what approximates a radically new antisemitic worldview.

RELIGIOUS INTOLERANCE

The oldest notions of Judeophobia were originally *religious* in character, and they predate Christianity. This does not mean that social prejudices and political concerns were absent. But it does mean that they were subservient to a form of religious outrage. Discrimination of various sorts may have existed, but it was not motivated by racial hatred or social resentment. The slavery endured by the Jews in Egypt was common to any number of peoples and it did not derive, primarily, from either economic motives or political fears. There was also little fear in Egypt, Greece, Rome, or during the Middle Ages that Jews were exerting undue political influence. Indeed, when outbreaks of violence against the Jews occurred in premodern times, they were rarely economically motivated and generally politically disorganized:[3] the primary motivation for such outbreaks was religious *belief.*

When the most fierce assaults were launched by Caligula in response to the Jewish riots of 38 CE in Alexandria, or when the Temple in Jerusalem was destroyed by the Romans in 70 CE, the enemy was not the Jewish people, but the Jewish religion and the Jewish way of life.[4] In other words, these cultures accepted *the Jew as a person, but not as a Jew.* Judaism was seen as an irritant in the broader culture; its members considered themselves different from their neighbors. An absolute clash of outlooks and practices, especially according to works like the *Protocols,* occurred from the very beginning [1A]. Jews understood themselves as the *chosen people* in the spirit of the covenant originally forged between Abraham and God. The distinction between Jews and others was established in the Biblical tale of Esau and Jacob.[5] It was then transformed into a new ethnic identity during the Exodus from Egypt, a signal event in the history of the Jews.

There is also more than one sense in which, from the standpoint of the Jews, history appears as a contest between idolatry and religion.[6] The fear of an invisible power, which works behind what is observable, would indeed become a mainstay of antisemitism and would surface in modern times in the guise of works like the *Protocols*

[1B]. The Jewish view on the origin of the world, in this same vein, was seen as undermining all other creation myths by dehumanizing their battles between gods, their heroic qualities, and their passion. In the beginning, for the Jews, there was only the *word*. The drama of birth was extinguished by a single demythologizing action in which God *said:* "Let there be light."[7]

The introduction of a single all-powerful God posed a challenge not merely to polytheism but to the reciprocity implicit in that form of belief. No longer would it become possible for every group to recognize the gods of others in return for the recognition of their own. The God of Israel was a jealous god who from the first, according to the *Protocols,* was intent on abolishing all religions other than those of the chosen people [14A]. The Jews certainly considered God more than *primus inter pares* or the first among equal gods: rather, worship of the Jewish God could not be compromised by worship of other, by definition false, gods. The arrogance of this stance was not lost on peoples with different beliefs: it indeed placed the Jews in a unique position against them and, undoubtedly, strengthened more mundane hatreds born of rival social and political interests. It is most likely the case that:

> Were it not for the intolerant attitude of the Jewish religion and the practices and culture dependent on it, there would have been little in Judaism to cause resentment toward the Jews who lived in various parts of the world. At the same time, however, had it not been for this very attitude, there probably would not be any Jews today. The other paradox is that the only thing that saved monotheistic Judaism was polytheistic paganism. Nonmonotheistic religions seem to have one magnanimous quality that Judaism, Christianity, Islam, etc. do not—an allowance for freedom of belief.[8]

The self-definition of the Jews as the people chosen by God, the *only* God, must surely have given them confidence and a sense of security. But it also undoubtedly triggered in non-Jews the profound feelings of fear and, perhaps unconsciously, the intense jealousy expressed in works like the *Protocols*. [22] The supposed inferiority of the Jews can indeed be understood as a psychological projection by the gentile whose gods are challenged and who does not feel as divinely favored. Jews were denounced in Egypt for refusing to recognize the divinity of the pharaoh. They were criticized in Greece and Rome for maintaining their insular form of community and separating themselves from the activities of the city-state *(polis)* and the "public space" *(res publica)* because both were tainted by pagan ritual. Jews were thus considered misanthropic and their private customs barbaric: Aristotle had said, after all, that the person "who is unable to share in the benefits of political association, or has no need to share because he is already self-sufficient . . . [is] either a beast or a god."[9]

The reason for the withdrawal of the Jews from public life stood beyond any immediate concern with discrimination or fears of being scapegoated. It was principally a matter of guaranteeing the survival of their culture. After the destruction of the Second Temple, which led to the expulsion of the Jews from Jerusalem, it was increasingly necessary to provide their cultural and religious life with its own unique and independent dynamic. And, in keeping with their faith, this needed to be done without idols or the structure of a hierarchical church. It was precisely their reliance upon the *Torah,* the emphasis they placed upon the "word," that enabled Jews to preserve their identity amid the most diverse cultures throughout what became known as the *diaspora.*[10]

Ironically, of course, Jews were usually criticized for ignoring public life by the very people who worked so hard to exclude them. But this resentment was surely inspired by a certain contempt for their beliefs and customs like circumcision. It also must have appeared the most rank form of superstition to pray to an invisible God incapable of being represented by idols. Jewish rituals were simply incomprehensible to most outsiders and cynics suspected something else was going on. Rumors spread: the Jews were accused of worshiping the head of a donkey made of gold; it was said they would not eat pork because they considered the pig divine; some suggested that they indulged in ritual murder and human sacrifice; others said that they practiced black magic.[11] Under the circumstances, of course, it was impossible to disprove such assertions. Jews had only the *word;* but their enemies realized that it had forged a deep and *invisible* bond. To the gullible, whether commoners or intellectuals, it only made sense that Jews should conspire with one another. Works like the *Protocols* would highlight this contention [2A, 13D].

Apion, Seneca, Tacitus, and other classical authors inveighed against the Jews. Wars against the Jewish people, discrimination, and isolated outbreaks of violence occurred among the Egyptians, the Greeks, the Romans. Jews may have been considered misguided, dogmatic, self-righteous, and misanthropic. But they were not seen as inherently evil. This would change after the rise of Christianity when rumors spread accusing the Jews of killing the Messiah. Mixed with a theory of the devil appropriated from the Persians, this rumor would turn into a historical myth with profound repercussions. All antisemitic works would highlight it: indeed, the *Protocols* identifies the Jews with a "symbolic snake" weaving its way around the world and inciting chaos by turning all forces against one another [3A]. The implied biblical reference to the story of Adam and Eve is obvious: Jews are to blame for the expulsion from Eden.

A new religion needs justification. Christianity did not start with a Jesus, but rather with the followers of several new and contending religious views in an age of complex political transitions and acute cultural conflict.[12] Certain intellectuals of the new faith responded to the upheaval in the first century by creatively fusing parables, adages, "pronouncements" *(logia),* tales of miracles, and Hebrew Scriptures into stories within a new and exceptionally beautiful poetic form. The result would ultimately become known as the New Testament.[13] As things stood, however, the old was dying and the new was not yet born. Significantly, there is much Greek and Jewish myth, folklore, and literary device present in the synoptic Gospels of Matthew, Mark, and Luke, as well as the book of John. Two folkloric traditions, in fact, underlie these Gospels: the Greek myth of the "noble death," which arguably begins with the execution of Socrates for heresy, and the Jewish myth of the persecuted sage, sometimes called the wisdom tale.[14] The former deals with the person willing to die for his

principles, while the latter concerns the victim of an unjust judgment, such as Esther or Daniel in the Old Testament, who is
threatened with death by a foreign despot only to be rescued when
the loyalty or piety of the person is discovered. The story of Christ is
firmly grounded in these two traditions.

The Gospel of Mark was the first to offer a life *(bios)* of Jesus. It
was written anonymously, as was the tradition, in the wake of the
Roman-Jewish war, approximately a half-century after Jesus' purported
death. Interestingly enough, it was only attributed to Mark two
centuries later.[15] It employed what little was known of the sayings and
stories from earlier traditions in the construction of an image of Jesus.
Fortified by an all-encompassing notion of human sin, which was itself
appropriated and reconstructed from Jewish theology by Paul, it
articulated what would become the basis for an "irrefutable" doctrine
of grace. The disciples of Jesus saw the importance of setting Jesus, the
prophet of *universal* love and forgiveness, against his own people. This
undertaking proved successful. Blaming the Jews for the death of
Christ, associating them with the inordinately powerful devil would
later become reinforced by the Church to the point where it entered
the collective unconscious of the gentile world. Nevertheless, these
themes were already articulated in the Gospels written under the spell
of the passion narrative for gentile audiences divorced from the
traditional Jewish way of life.

Satan already had begun to assume importance among the
followers of Jesus in the century following his death. The Gospel of
Mark introduced the devil into the opening scene enabling the
ministry of Jesus to become defined by its willingness to engage in a
continual struggle between the spirit of God and those who belong
to the "kingdom" of his adversary. Placing Jesus in conflict not only
with the scribes and the Pharisees, but also with the Jewish priests,
the Sadducees, gave a new twist to the Jewish tradition of the
"persecuted sage." It enabled the writer to depict the Jews as
conspiring to kill Jesus on not only religious but political grounds; it
also, however, made room for the introduction of the Greek notion
of the noble death. The supposed manipulation of the Romans by
the Jews in bringing about the crucifixion of Jesus set the stage for

charges in works like the *Protocols* that the Jews were manipulating the Freemasons for nefarious purposes [4A]. It would matter little that the "facts" of the original story are inconsistent with both Jewish and Roman law as documented at the time: an execution held on Passover would have been an outrage and the failure of the witnesses to agree would have resulted in a mistrial under Roman law.[16]

The other Gospels, whose true authors also remain unknown, retain anti-Jewish sentiments. But they are somewhat less dramatic and severe in the character of their prejudice. Their importance lies in the ways they indicate that the spirit of God no longer belongs strictly to the Jews, but to all peoples. The Gospel of Matthew is often considered a document of "Jewish Christianity," compiled by members of a Christian sect that did not survive the rising tide of Christian orthodoxy in the fourth century, which succeeds in appropriating the Jewish Scriptures as the "old testament." The Gospel of Luke, written between 70 and 80 CE, turns Jesus into a transitional figure: indeed, with eyes now turned toward the gentiles, He stands between the God of Israel and the new Christian God.[17] The decisive step is taken by the Gospel of John, however, which experts have dated sometime between 90 and 150 CE. The traditional Jewish conception of the word *(logos)*, is now transferred from the Hebrew God to Jesus himself in the famous lines: "And the Word was made flesh, and dwelt among us, and we beheld his glory, the glory as the only begotten son of the Father, full of grace and truth" (John 1:14). The old is now severed from the new: the Jews remain in darkness while the Christians enter the light.

The four Gospels, chosen by the Church from hundreds of contradictory and internally inconsistent accounts of the Christ figure, would shape the Christian perspective of Jews in a profound manner. Through these works, whatever their literary and even emancipatory value, Christians eventually "absorbed, along with the quite contrary sayings of Jesus, the association between the forces of evil and Jesus' Jewish enemies. Whether illiterate or sophisticated, those who heard the gospel stories, or saw them illustrated in their churches, generally assumed both their historical accuracy and their religious validity."[18]

Christianity has given birth to an infinite variety of interpretations. Identifying it with antisemitism simply and solely is inaccurate
and misleading. There is no denying, however, that the myth of
Jewish culpability grew in concert with the growth in institutional
dominance of the Catholic Church in Rome. Its representatives
insisted Christ was the Savior and that the Jews, whose religion had
no place for the "Son of God," killed him: the chosen people were
believed to have been chosen less by God than the devil from whom
they derived the power to realize their ends. This myth became
intertwined with the notion that Jesus had come with a message of
universal salvation rejected by the Jews. They were seen as obstinately
clinging to the *word* of the Torah rather than embracing the *passion*
of the Savior. Jewish commitment to the word rather than the spirit
helped inspire the creation of Christianity and its separation from
Judaism in which its Messiah grew to maturity.

Problems presented themselves, however, for the new religion.
Christians found themselves forced to explain why their message was
not being accepted by the majority of Jews and, simultaneously, why
they should wield political influence in the crumbling Roman
Empire.[19] There could obviously be nothing wrong with the divine
message itself and so, logically, there must be something wrong with
its recipient. This point is driven home in the story of Barabbas and
Christ. According to Matthew, when told by Pontius Pilate to choose
between them, the Jewish mob called for the release of Barabbas. As
for Christ, its members rendered the judgment: "Let him be cruci-
fied"(Matt. 27:22). Pilate then washed his hands and said: "I am
innocent of the blood of this just person. See ye to it" (27:24). This
was when the Jewish mob supposedly cried: "His blood be upon us
and our children" (27:25). The situation was clear for the adherents
of the new religion: the Jews had willfully and consciously demanded
the execution of Christ while the unwitting and ultimately guilt-
ridden Romans merely acted as their agents.

Whether any of this actually took place is questionable. Mark
speaks of Barabbas committing a murder while participating in a
Jewish insurrection (15:7). But, interestingly enough, Barabbas was
not a proper name. It is instead probably a mistranslation of the

Aramaic phrase "bar abba," which means either "son of the father" or "son of God," by the Greek writers of the Gospels.[20] There is also no evidence substantiating the assertion that a choice was ever made between a man named Barabbas and another named Jesus. Whether true or merely another rumor about the Jews, however, the consequences of this morality tale proved of enormous significance: responsibility for the death of Jesus shifted from the Romans to the Jews, compromise with the Christ-killers became anathema, and an alliance between Christians and the Roman Empire emerged as a realistic possibility.

With the conversion of Constantine in 313 CE, and his appointment as sole emperor of the Roman Empire following a bloody coup in 324, Christianity became the official religion of the empire. This event triggered the systemic organization of the Christian faith: dogma was established, churches were built, ritual was regularized, and salvation made eternal. Augustine even argued in *The City of God* that political institutions could serve as servants of the Lord if they furthered the predominance of the Christian religion and rooted out its enemies. The circle closed: Jews became the enemies of Christ and the newly powerful Church would only serve its God by punishing them.

"The wounds of a friend are better than the kisses of an enemy," wrote Augustine, and this less than ambiguous statement would soon be used to justify abolishing the taboo against killing. Complete obedience to the Church soon became the order of the day: pagan knowledge antithetical to Christian teachings was banned, heretics were murdered, the dogma of the "true faith" was forged, and a vast bureaucracy was created. The Church became intent on eradicating the devil and all his works, and the world fell into a stretch of illiteracy and ignorance that would last nearly a thousand years. From the torrent of antisemitic pogroms during the eleventh century in Rouen, Orleans, Limoges, Mainz, and other cities along the Rhine, to the Inquisition begun in 1231 under the reign of Pope Gregory IX against heretics and infidels, the guiding motivation for the slaughter was: "God wills it!"[21]

And why did "God will it?" Half-forgotten fanatics like St. John Chrysostom, Bishop of Constantinople in the fourth century, as well as the more famous ones of later generations like Melanchthon and Martin Luther, kept the old memories of Jewish iniquity and the old fears of Jewish satanism alive among the common people. Christian baptism still requires the willingness to "renounce the Devil and all his works." Only two possible reasons could plausibly exist why anyone would persist in rejecting salvation: ignorance of the fact that "Christ died for our sins" (1Cor. 15:3) or a willful refusal to acknowledge the "truth." The *ignorant* could be taught the truth: most people believed that putting obstacles in the way of practicing the Jewish faith, prohibiting synagogues from being repaired, or subjecting Jews to unfair taxation, would further the eradication of Judaism and its "erroneous" teachings.[22] With the *willfully evil,* however, it was another matter: it would only be logical to assume that they were engaged in a battle against Christianity in which, as the *Protocols* suggest, they would use any means expedient to the end [1C,D]. The faithful must therefore rid the world of them by either expulsion or death.

Coexistence with the Jews was always a purely tactical matter for the Christian zealot: conversion or worse were the only genuine alternatives for Jews in the Middle Ages. The Church quickly realized, however, that anyone can go through the rituals of conversion without *really* undergoing it at all. Its officials considered it impossible to trust those in league with the devil. Suspicions of this sort would also ideologically justify the infamous Spanish Inquisition in 1480. This inquisition was introduced by royal order since it served to increase the powers of a burgeoning nation state and a new form of absolute monarchy over disparate localities and a recalcitrant populace. But the Church, of course, also derived benefits. The Inquisition was a source of revenue for its officials who often kept the wealth plundered from the accused and garnered bribes from the wealthy hoping to avoid accusation.[23] It was an efficient way to deal with "false Christians," or *Marranos,* who had been driven to baptism in the preceding century. It also guaranteed conformity amid the turbulence and outbreaks of heterodoxy during the High Middle Ages.

Associating Jews with the devil made them the embodiment of supernatural forces and dangerous to the truly God-fearing. The suspicion of heresy was never lifted from the Jews: there were always rumors of strange rituals being practiced, dangerous plots being hatched and black magic being employed in order to bring about the triumph of the devil. This was not merely the case in Spain where the Inquisition would last until 1834 by finding new targets: heretics, witches, and other critics of the Church.[24] Luther, too, refused to take any chances. Thus, he called for exerting punishment upon

> . . . persons who would only appear to be godly, or commit secret sins.
> Such were the Jews, and such too are all hypocrites, for they live
> without joy and love. In their hearts, they hate the divine law and, as
> is the way with all hypocrites, they habitually condemn others. They
> regard themselves as spotless, although they are full of envy, hatred,
> pride, and all kinds of impurity, [Matthew 23 :28]. These are precisely
> the people who despise God's goodness, and heap up the divine wrath
> by their hardness of heart.[25]

Late modernization in Spain and the attempt of its bureaucratic institutions to maintain their existence clearly counted as causes for the long survival of the Inquisition. Especially in this most catholic of nations, however, the charge of heresy against Jews justified the need for vigilance and the maintenance of the Inquisition. Just as the devil had been left on earth as an admonition and temptation for the righteous, it was argued, God had left the Jews on earth in order to show that the gentiles were not responsible for the murder of Christ. Indeed since the first century, this juxtaposition of the grace of God with the spirit of Satan vindicated the followers of Jesus and demonized their enemies.

The Jew could not be like the Christian; thus, the fabrication of the *other* began. It was widely believed in the Renaissance that Jewish males menstruated, for example, which served as one explanation for the famous "blood libel"; the belief that Jews murdered Christian children and consumed their blood in the matzos made for Passover, to replenish the blood lost in menstruation,[26] was still accepted by various circles in Imperial Russia when the *Protocols* made its appearance. A bit later the Jew would become identified with the vampire:[27] without a homeland, wandering the world, the Jew is like the vampire who carries with him his coffin partially filled with the soil of his homeland. In the popular imagination, like the vampire, the Jewish "bloodsucker" fortifies himself with the blood of Christians and especially Christian virgins; he, too, is mortally afraid of the cross. The vampire communicates with others of his breed and there in the darkness, like the Jew, he hatches the conspiracy described in the *Protocols* against the Christian community [7]. Images and myths of this sort did not die with the advent of modernity. Even today, on the Internet, an antisemitic group can defend the *Protocols* by claiming that in order to understand the conspiracy to take over the world,

> we must first realize that Satan is real and that he is at war with God. This being the case, it would be strange indeed if there were no conspiracy dreamed up by him to rule the world, using human agents ... [and] the Talmudic system of Jewry plays a prominent role in this plan.[28]

The images and myths of times past became transformed to meet the needs of succeeding generations. Remnants of the past were carried over into modernity: precapitalist classes struggled against the new capitalist system; aristocrats and the *petit bourgeoisie* battled first the monarchical nation-state and then its republican incarnation; and, finally, religious institutions fought the Enlightenment whose proponents were often themselves scarred with outworn prejudices. There is nothing pure about progress. The antimodern reaction was built into modernity from the very beginning and helped shape its development. Older forms of antisemitism thereby became reconfigured in the new context. The scapegoat changed its face.

Untold courageous acts in defense of Jews were committed by Christians with a conscience. But the darker side of Christian history is undeniable and it is appalling that only in the late twentieth century under Pope John Paul II should the Church have chosen to condemn the "misunderstandings" of the past and the "misinterpretations" of Scripture. Christians misunderstand themselves and misinterpret their own history when they view the persecution suffered by the Jews in these terms. Official theology was, in fact, traditionally less antisemitic than the popular myths about the Jews; this is perhaps why standard histories of Christian doctrine have said relatively little about the palpable reality of Christian hostility to the Jews. But, though antisemitism might have been a product of the popular mind, it was surely reinforced by church theologians fanatical in their beliefs and their hatreds. Indeed, if those in the age of enlightenment "formed an imaginary image of Jewish race, they did so because a theologically condemned caste already existed."[29]

SOCIAL PREJUDICE

This "condemned caste" of Jews mostly longed for modernity. The political vision of most educated Jews was precise and inspired by their hatred of a very simple proposition articulated by St. Ambrose: "civil law must bow before religious devotion." The feudal subordination of law to the Christian religion put Jews at an obvious disadvantage. They responded by identifying with the new monarchical state whose centralized legal system provided the foundations for modern liberal democracies.[30] Jews wanted to be seen as individuals with equal rights under the liberal rule of law. Shakespeare put it beautifully when his caricature of a Jew, Shylock, speaks against the prejudices of other characters and probably those of the author as well in *The Merchant of Venice:*

> I am a Jew. Hath not a Jew eyes? Hath not a Jew hands, organs, dimensions, senses, affections, passions? Fed with the same food, hurt with the same weapons, subject to the same diseases, healed by the same means, warmed and cooled by the same winter and summer, as a Christian is? If you prick us, do we not bleed? If you tickle us, do we not laugh? If you poison us, do we not die? And if you wrong us, shall we not revenge? If we are like you in the rest, we will resemble you in that. (Act III, Scene 1)

If the Jews did not invent the Enlightenment [1E], or bring about the great revolutions instituting republicanism [3D], as charged in the *Protocols,* then they undoubtedly should have. They were the disenfranchised, burdened with centuries of discriminatory laws and practices. The great majority of Jews were dirt-poor and they lived in overcrowded ghettos nothing like the sentimentalized portrayal in *Fiddler on the Roof.* Associating Jews with the Rothschilds and the Guggenheims, or simply with the holders of great wealth as the *Protocols* do [6A], is a historical distortion. They constituted a community within a community, a nation within a nation, and what the philosopher Johann Gottlieb Fichte called a "state within a state." Most gentiles were probably less concerned with justice for the Jews than bringing an end to what was often termed a "plague on the nation" by abolishing Judaism through assimilation. Ultimately, however, their motivation was irrelevant. More important was the clear recognition that things could not remain the way they were.

"Emancipation" from the legacies of the feudal past became a concern for farsighted state-builders like the Austrian emperor Joseph II and democrats everywhere.[31] It began during the Enlightenment of the eighteenth century; it created intense opposition during the nineteenth century, and, in certain states, extended well into the twentieth century. The emancipation of the Jews was part of the attempt to create a new bourgeois society of "constitutions and machines," as a slogan of the time put the matter, and liquidate the *ancien régime:* the aristocracy and the landed estates, the Church, and the other remnants of feudalism. It basically attempted to bring Jews into public life through the introduction of a flexible notion of nationalism profoundly connected with the republican idea.[32] The walls of the ghetto would crumble, social professions would open, and Jews would finally claim their rights as equal citizens.

The crowning achievements of this emancipatory enterprise were the American Revolution of 1776 and the French Revolution of 1789. Constitutionalism was instituted and the long struggle for suffrage began. These revolutions were predicated on the vision of a new order in which equal citizens of diverse backgrounds and different interests would determine their fate together peacefully under the liberal rule of law [10A].[33] Constitutionalism and suffrage rejected the idea of individuals living without explicit human rights in a community bound together by land and custom. It indeed made sense that Jews should have welcomed these developments. But the antisemites were furious; works like the *Protocols* called the constitution a "school of discords" [10A], and its supporters believed that parliamentary institutions based on suffrage served merely to hide the play of Jewish interests and Jewish control over the new industrial society [10B].

But, ironically, even the more secular Jews did not have an easy time of it. Those concerned with securing the rights of their brethren, breaking down the walls of the ghetto, and introducing them to the general society came up against the barriers of religious and cultural tradition both outside and inside their community. Emancipation involved freeing Jews both from the wider feudal past and from their own ghetto cultures in a capricious world where the continuing power of the former generally did not permit a complete break with the latter. There were also enough Jews who opposed the undertaking. These included orthodox traditionalists as well as members of the newly formed *Hasidim,* who sought to liberate the spirit by rendering holy the affairs of everyday life. There were also political conservatives with a stake in the status quo and small-minded provincials who sought their safety in the ghetto. Opposition to the modernizing spirit of the *Haskalah* or the Enlightenment was strongest in Eastern Europe and in the less economically developed areas of western nations. Nevertheless, in cities like Berlin, this spirit took hold among professionals, businessmen, and intellectuals; it would soon capture the majority of the western Jewish community.

Jews like Moses Mendelssohn and his gentile friend Gotthold Ephraim Lessing, author of the celebrated play *Nathan the Wise* with its famous plea for tolerance, instituted a virtual revolution. Leaders of the *Haskalah* called upon Jews to enter the world. Mendelssohn himself was observant of religious custom. But he and his followers certainly made easier the abandonment of religious tradition through their emphasis on secular values and participation in the wider world of the burgeoning nation-state. Jews immediately took advantage of the possibilities offered by liberal society, and this resulted in a profound change in their sense of identity: they became secular, moved out of the ghetto, increased their contact with gentiles, and sought advancement. Antisemitic works like the *Protocols* would view this change as just another way to make Christians dependent upon Jews for their daily bread and thereby subordinate them [13A].

Many Jews, especially among the ambitious and the educated, were baptized: the renowned scholar, and future teacher of Karl Marx, Eduard Gans; the great literary figure, who thought of becoming a lawyer, Heinrich Heine; the fascinating Rahel Varnhagen, whose salon was home to so many leading intellectual personalities of the time; and others. Most made their choice on practical grounds, like Gans who converted in order to secure his chair of philosophy at the University of Berlin. But others felt what Heine called the "betrayal complex" or, like Varnhagen, remained preoccupied with their Jewishness until their death. This trend toward baptism in the nineteenth century indeed began the process of identifying "the Jew" less by religion than by other attributes. Jews lost the sense of security and belonging offered by the ghetto. They entered the world as individuals and, in the process, loosened the bonds tying together the community. Indeed, if only for this reason, Mendelssohn and the leading figures of the *Haskalah* have fallen into disfavor among religious conservatives, postmodernists, and Zionists alike.

Those concerned with issues of "identity" raise the objection that the proponents of Enlightenment and the liberal state accepted the Jew only as a person, but not as a Jew.[34] The liberal state was too weak, or hypocritical, to protect its most despised minority, and the old hatreds blossomed. Therein seemingly lies the failure of emancipation and the source of what would become the genocide of the twentieth century. But this position rests on a set of profound historical and philosophical misunderstandings. The real issue attendant upon the age of emancipation was not the unwillingness of reactionary gentiles to accept the Jew as a Jew: it was rather, in contrast to the religious intolerance of the premodern age, *their unwillingness to accept the Jew as a person endowed with rights equal to those of the non-Jew.*

The history of antisemitism attests to the superiority of the Anglo-American over the continental understanding of liberalism. The constitutional liberalism fashioned primarily in England and the United States during the seventeenth and eighteenth century by figures like John Locke, Thomas Jefferson, and Thomas Paine is markedly different from the continental liberalism of the nineteenth century inspired by figures like Fichte, Ernest Renan, and Friedrich Meinecke. Constitutional liberalism was fundamentally unconcerned with issues of national identity. It sought, in the first instance, to protect the individual from the arbitrary exercise of political authority and to separate church from state; its primary aim was to prevent old forms of religiously inspired civil wars by granting all citizens equality regardless of their backgrounds or customs or convictions.[35] Thus, in principle, Jews and others would be able to act as citizens and still maintain their customs and religion.

Continental liberalism was far less individualistic and far more inclined toward an exclusivist, inflexible, and emotive form of nationalism or what Rousseau originally termed a "civic religion."[36] Its advocates retained a certain romantic commitment to the idea of a homogeneous "people's state" *(Volksstaat),* and they often aligned themselves with authoritarian state builders like Bismarck. Some like Fichte deified the German *Volk* and considered nationalism as the equivalent of revealed religion; it was almost logical for him to claim that "the only way to give [Jews] citizenship would be to cut off their heads on the same night in order to replace them with those containing no Jewish ideas."[37]

Other continental liberals were less rhetorical: this becomes evident in the famous antisemitism controversy *(Antisemitismusstreit)* of 1879 between Heinrich von Treitschke and Theodor Mommsen in which the former stressed the undue influence of Jews on German society, called upon Jews to become more "German," and introduced the phrase that would become a popular slogan under the Nazis:

"The Jews are our misfortune!" *(Die Juden sind unser Unglück!)*. Such views fundamentally contradict the premises of constitutional liberalism. Indeed, they only attest to the lack of a genuinely liberal tradition in Germany and other nations where antisemitism played an important political role.

In the shadow of the holocaust and amid lingering memories of the failed Weimar Republic, which Hitler trampled on the road to power, postwar scholars showed themselves increasingly skeptical about liberal solutions to the "Jewish question": they looked to Germany in order to explain the "failure" of emancipation.[38] But, in fact, this notion proves emblematic only of those in which the liberal "emancipation" of Jews was attempted without the existence of attendant liberal political institutions, liberal traditions, or a sense of the "dignity of man" inherited from the Renaissance. Emancipation was undertaken gradually in Germany, step by legislative step, with varying degrees of success in a mosaic of mostly reactionary principalities where radically different numbers of Jews lived. Germany was not even a nation in the beginning of the nineteenth century and the lateness of its constitution as a state generated what would remain an assorted set of problems associated with its national identity.[39] The liberal assumptions embraced by supporters of "emancipation" cannot be judged by the results, more than a century later, in what was still notably an "illiberal society."[40]

The "Jewish question" became a question only in nations where progressive social forces committed to constitutional liberalism and capitalism were confronted with strong reactionary social forces committed to the hierarchical and Christian vision of a feudal past. This becomes evident in the *Protocols* [4B]. Emancipation was not an issue of any practical importance in the United States and, at the other extreme, it was not even a matter for discussion in Imperial Russia. In nations with liberal institutions and liberal traditions, such as the United States or England or the Netherlands, emancipation was basically successful. It makes as little sense to speak about the failure of Jewish emancipation in nations lacking liberal institutions and values as it does to speak about the failure of marxian socialism in economically underdeveloped nations lacking a proletariat.

Critics of emancipation would note how, during the French Revolution, Clermont Tonnerre argued that the aim of the new society was to liberate Jews as individuals rather than liberate Jewry.[41] But this criticism misunderstands the purpose of even the more radical form of constitutional liberalism. It offered individuals freedom from the arbitrary interference of the state in their private lives and equality under the law, not "group rights"; it sought to turn each individual into a capitalist, not to abolish capitalism; it offered formal equality under the law of the state, not substantive equality in the realm of civil society. Marx saw these defects as warranting the move beyond "political emancipation" and toward "human emancipation" in his early work *The Jewish Question,* which employs antisemitic terminology and contains antisemitic overtones.[42]

Written prior to the development of his theory of history and his famous analysis of capitalism, *The Jewish Question* associated the new economic system with Jewish attributes: Marx built on an economic motivation for antisemitism inherited from the Middle Ages when, following the Third Lateran Council of 1179, Christians were prohibited from charging interest and Jews were placed in the position of serving as moneylenders in an agrarian society. The antisemitic characterizations used by Marx were common among intellectuals of the period. More striking was the lack of any institutional referent for his notion of "human emancipation" compared with the idea of "political emancipation" predicated on the existence of a republic. This same vagueness is apparent on the part of those who called for the "emancipation of Jewry" or, like Treitschke, for making Jews more German. Advocates of these dissimilar concerns indeed shared a marked inability to offer concrete institutional or programmatic proposals.

Historically and logically, everywhere, the success of the struggle for Jewish emancipation ran parallel with the fortunes of constitutional liberalism.[43] Often, initially, only Christian males with property were granted full citizenship and the right to vote. But constitutional liberalism was predicated on universal principles of formal equality and reciprocity. The liberal rule of law made it possible to question particular discriminatory laws and practices or intolerant calls to surrender personal beliefs and customs. This is precisely what antisemites and reactionaries hated about the new order initiated by the Enlightenment, formulated during the democratic revolutions, and unevenly spread throughout Europe by Napoleon.

Emancipation into the broader society was the hope of the Jews. Organizing themselves in terms of their "identity" was nowhere a viable political option: Zionism was itself a "post-emancipation" phenomenon with little intellectual or mass support before the last quarter of the nineteenth century. The liberal vision of emancipation offered the sole serious possibility for bettering the lives of Jews in the historical context of the eighteenth and nineteenth centuries. The Jews knew it and proponents of the antisemitic reaction knew it as well. The champions of liberal democracy fought for it and the counterrevolutionary enemies of liberal democracy fought against it. Critics of emancipation, blinded by matters of identity, focus on the wrong target. The primary problem was not the *proponents* of emancipation who recognized "the Jew as a person, but not as a Jew"; the problem was instead the *opponents* of emancipation who refused to recognize the Jew as an autonomous human being endowed with rights under the law.

Works like the *Protocols* would turn "the Jew" into the agent for what, in another context, Max Weber termed the "disenchantment of the world." But with a certain proviso: While Jewish philosophers, or those in the service of Jews, supposedly exposed the shortcomings of Christianity, they never dared betray the allegedly mystical secrets of Judaism [14B]. In any event, with their corrosive rationalism and their "arithmetical" skills, Jews were criticized for undermining traditional society and anticipating the modern system they so adeptly dominated according to the *Protocols* [4B]. Antisemites saw them as manipulating gullible if honest Christians through the new liberal state and its attendant institutions in order to assure the undisputed authority of the "learned elders of Zion" [13C]. Because Freemasons admitted Jews into some of their lodges, which repression had driven underground, it seemed obvious that the two groups were in league with one another: after all, obviously in keeping with their allies, the Freemasons also employed the six-pointed star as a mysterious symbol in their mythology. The Jews may have sought to assimilate within the broader society, in short, but for the antisemites they remained outsiders intent on disrupting the organic and homogeneous peasant community [5A].

The years following the Napoleonic Wars were dominated by attempts to introduce a "restoration" of precisely this form of community. Stendhal appropriately called the period, stretching from 1815 to 1848, a "swamp"; it was dominated by the army and the Church or, using the title of his most famous work, "the red and the black." Antisemitism and the romantic ideology of this self-proclaimed counterrevolution shared a profound and transparent connection. Both were directed against everything associated with the Enlightenment and the French Revolution. They sought to replace the primacy once accorded reason with intuition. Christianity was resurrected, so to speak, in order to contest the earlier trend toward secularism.[44] Aristocratic tradition and religious authority were, as remains the case in the *Protocols,* the responses to "freedom of conscience" [17].

This restoration philosophy of an outraged church and a dispossessed aristocracy was the expression of a romantic assault on modernity in general and republicanism in particular. Its proponents rejected the idea of equality in favor of an aristocratic notion of "rank" and feared the subversion of hierarchy. These concerns would carry over into the *Protocols* [9,10,16]. The restoration embraced the notion of a universal church and a single true religion with universal validity. But its advocates rejected universalist ideas regarding the secular rights of "man and citizen" in favor of nationalist forms of particularism and they sought to abolish the political gains recently granted the Jews. Joseph de Maistre was among the leading lights of the counterrevolution and, in this vein, he noted with his renowned wit that:

The Constitution of 1795, just like its predecessors, was made for *man.* But there is no such thing as *man* in the world. In the course of my life I have seen Frenchmen, Italians, Russians, etc.; I know, too, thanks to Montesquieu, *that one can be a Persian.* But as for *man,* I declare that I have never met him in my life; if he exists, he is unknown to me.[45]

This mundane observation is now quoted by progressive thinkers to justify an assault on universals and a politics based on identity.[46] It is too often forgotten, however, that with the attack on universals comes the attack on liberal notions of right and the republican ideal of the citizen. This rejection of natural rights and human dignity, which the Enlightenment inherited from the Renaissance, was the motor for transforming hatred of the Jew into a distinctly social prejudice during the early nineteenth century.

Advocates of this position believed that "Jewish trade" was harmful to civil society.[47] They came from many classes. Aristocrats looked down upon the Jewish parvenus; peasants hated the "Jewish" bankers who charged them interest for their loans; small merchants lashed out against the owners of the new "Jewish" department stores; religious provincials noted with growing alarm the influx of Jews into the educational establishment; nationalists worried about the influence of Jews upon the proletariat and their role in the burgeoning labor movement. All these groups inimically opposed progress, urbanization, parliamentarism, and the new capitalist society of anonymous individuals held together by what Marx termed the "cash nexus." Works like the *Protocols* reflected the interest of the *losers* in the great battle between the forces of modernity and the forces of tradition [6]. Indeed, the sense of despair about modernity would ultimately prove more important than the empirical class background of individuals in explaining the attraction of antisemitism in modern life.

The Christian could no longer *recognize* the Jew in modern society: Jews lived in the city with its anonymity, received their diplomas, entered the tertiary sector, participated in commerce and exchange, became journalists, engaged in liberal and socialist politics, and played an important role among the "critical intelligentsia."[48] Jews were increasingly visible as individual representatives of particular political and cultural trends but invisible as a group. Antisemites, for their part, found themselves needing ever more surely to fix their enemy with some set of determinants. As Jews rid themselves of their traditional garb and their religious habits, and entered civil society, characterizing Jews as a race became an ever stronger temptation.

A new expression of Judeophobic ideology had already made its appearance in 1815 when a "purity of race" program was developed by the extreme wing of youthful German nationalism. The point was not simply to establish hierarchical relations of superiority and inferiority or even to create perverse stereotypes. Racism was instead employed, against the universalist principles of Enlightenment political theory, to justify the *rishes* of the antisemite and provide reasons why Jews could not assimilate into the nation. It sought to show why Jews were *not* people like other people and capable of participating equally in Christian society: indeed, precisely because Jews were seen as constituting an organic "race" or "nation," it followed that non-Jews must begin identifying themselves in the same way. Only through racial consciousness would it be possible to recognize the Jewish threat. And so, depending upon the context, "the Jew" would be pitted against "the French" or "the Aryan." Those who ignored this ineradicable conflict between Jews and gentiles were obviously traitors to the nation or the race.

Such thinking was in the air when, just as the debates over Jewish emancipation were taking place in Germany, the "Hep-Hep" pogroms broke out in 1819.[49] They spread throughout southern and eastern Germany, causing loss of property and lives, fueled by what demagogues called the "anger of the people." A new form of right-wing protest was crystallizing. It only simmered in the next three decades following the pogroms: the old aristocratic reaction remained dominant. But the new form burst forth in the decades following the Revolutions of 1848 which, essentially, sought to make good the unfulfilled promises of 1789.[50] These uprisings sought to establish republican institutions and social justice. The ensuing reaction ultimately brought figures like Napoleon III and Bismarck to power even as it generated a new commitment to integral nationalism and the organic community.

Ideological notions of this sort inspired the rise of populist movements led by powerful figures like Karl Lueger,[51] who would become the longstanding mayor of Vienna, and Adolf Stoecker, the court chaplain of Kaiser Wilhelm I in Berlin. Literary figures in France like Maurice Barrès worried about their nation becoming "deracinated" while in Austria during the last quarter of the nineteenth century Georg Ritter von Schönerer—among the leaders of the staunchly authoritarian and antisemitic German national movement and an idol of the young Hitler—was already successfully employing the slogans "Germany for the Germans" and "From Purity to Unity."[52]

Important political activists like these retained their contempt for the Jewish religion. But while concerned with building a Christian national community,[53] their movements were primarily fueled by social prejudice or *rishes*. They ran candidates for office and they were generally very careful never to threaten the existing political order. Their often radical rhetoric and outlandish symbolic actions against liberals and Jews stood in marked contrast to their actual demands. Their aims were crystallized in the famous Petition of 1880 in Germany that gathered 265,000 signatures: it sought to limit Jewish immigration, exclude Jews from high governmental positions, introduce a special census to keep track of Jews, and prohibit the hiring of Jews as elementary school teachers.[54]

Anti-Jewish measures of this sort were too tame to meet the needs of antisemites in the next century. Wilhelm Marr may have introduced the term "antisemitism" in 1879 to differentiate his new and more political Judeophobia from its predecessors.[55] But the theory outstripped the practice. The politicians of hate were still enmeshed in the more traditional ideology. Old-fashioned bigots like Lueger and Stoecker initially tried to present themselves as "peaceful" advocates of Christian social reform in contrast to an atheistic, secular, and revolutionary social democracy. They lacked an overriding critique of parliamentarism and they refused to break with Christian symbolism. They were still too bound by establishmentarian concerns and they rejected violence. They were indeed unwilling to do what needed to be done.

Many elements of Nazism appear in these early movements: the cult of the leader, the racist attitude against Jews, the anti-intellectual populism, and the extravagant nationalism. In antisemitic terms, however, their racism no less than their general programs were too diffuse. When Eugen Dühring began promulgating his violent antisemitism inside the German labor movement, which was part of a more general attempt to introduce an irrational populism and a new theory celebrating violence, Friedrich Engels made the official position of social democracy clear in his proletarian best-seller *Anti-Dühring*.[56] It would soon enough become common for members of the labor movement to claim that "anti-semitism is the socialism of idiots" *(der Sozialismus des dummen Kerls)*. In Europe, generally speaking, the failure to attract a significant working-class base for Judeophobia produced the need for a new approach.

Just as religious intolerance made way for social prejudice, social prejudice began to make way for a political antisemitism directed not merely against Jews, but against the quintessentially modern world they supposedly dominated. World War I finally eliminated aristocratic politics with its catholic vision as an alternative to the liberal state and the capitalist economy. Antisemitic ideology would have to take a different form in dealing with both the historical crisis and the Jew whom they considered responsible. A new assault on the *world* of modernity would set the stage for genocide: in contrast to the Judeophobia of earlier times, it presupposed a denial of the Jew *both* as a person *and* as a Jew. With a nostalgic view of the past and a sense of despair about the future, the *Protocols* helped initiate this new form of political antisemitism by identifying the most progressive trends of modernity with what became known as the "Jewish spirit."

POLITICAL ANTISEMITISM

The *Protocols* unifies the religious, the social, and the political elements of Judeophobia in a particularly striking way. It expresses the resentment of a Christian world against the undermining of its faith and it seeks to close public life to the Jews. But it is no longer principally concerned with either the betrayal of the "true faith," the rollback of rights, or the connection of Jews with this or that movement in this or that nation. An all-embracing perspective on the Jews emerges in which the sum of their evil becomes more than its parts: the Jew now appears as the devil in a modern guise. Pulling the strings behind the scenes, dominating the new system of modernity, the Jew becomes the cause of every catastrophe. Antisemitism is no longer predicated on the idea of Jews blocking the end of days, standing in the way of paradise, or even dominating this or that profession. The Jew has conquered history and the Jewish spirit has invaded every part of modern life. Antisemites must deal with a new situation: it has become incumbent upon them to eliminate the "Jewish spirit" which, in contrast to previous forms of Judeophobia, calls for denying the Jew both as a person and as a Jew.

The *Protocols* made Judeophobia part of a more "total," and distinctly modern, form of political antimodernism: it crystallized the idea of the Jew as scapegoat. The traditional religious hatred of Jews and the social fears about their economic gains remained intact. But the Jews were now viewed as engaged in a Promethean enterprise. Works like the *Protocols* claimed that they were planning the overthrow of the most rigid expressions of feudal despotism in order to set up their own far worse form of tyranny [15D]. An international conspiracy of Jews directed by their leading "elder of Zion" was considered intent on taking political power by any means necessary including torture, starvation, and the inoculation of diseases [10C]. Chaos loomed and civilization itself was at stake. The Grand Rabbi's hand was everywhere calling upon his flock to engage in "confirming the dynastic roots of King David to the last strata of the earth" [24].

This global antisemitic vision developed as the nineteenth century came to a close. A false image still exists of life during the *fin de siècle*. It is captured in the wonderful paintings of the impressionists and early postimpressionists with their glorification of everyday life and the literary works reflecting the calm, innocent, and ordered "world of yesterday" (Stefan Zweig). It was indeed a time of relative peace and incredible technological development. But this period was framed by the economic crash of 1873 in Europe and the great financial crisis of

1898 in Russia that only threw the material insecurity of the masses into sharper relief. The *fin de siècle* was marked by anti-Jewish riots in France, state-sponsored pogroms in Russia and Eastern Europe, the emergence of new antisemitic political parties and movements in Austria and Germany, as well as a rising tide of imperialism, militarism, and chauvinism. The "good years" were not that good and, for all the success the Jews achieved in the new industrial society, *la belle époque* was not that beautiful for the Jews.

In earlier times, Jews were hated for divorcing themselves from public life. In the modern world, however, they were increasingly castigated for controlling what Jürgen Habermas termed the public sphere or the complex of institutions in which "public opinion" [7B] is forged:[57] Works like the *Protocols* claimed that the Jews had established themselves in the universities [16A], the educational system [16B], the press [12A], and all organs of public debate protected by civil liberties [9D]. Richard Wagner even condemned the Jews for their insidious control of music in what became his most popular literary effort, *The Jewish Element in Music* (1849). They would soon become identified with the avant-garde trends in literature and painting, or what the Nazis termed cultural Bolshevism *(Kulturbolschewismus)*. Indeed, the modern Czech novelist Milan Kundera was correct when he noted that Jews were the "intellectual cement of middle-European culture." Antisemitic journals pilloried Jews as much for their public influence [2C] as for supposedly initiating and benefiting from the economic turmoil. The term "civilized Jew" *(Zivilisationsjude)* actually acquired a certain fashionable insult-value toward the close of the nineteenth century.

Antisemitic works like the *Protocols* began to exhibit an almost pathological fear of any attempt to "debilitate the public mind" [15D]. They worried over the decline of morality and the national "spirit." Parliamentarism, elections, political parties, and economic competition came under attack. The *Protocols* argued that education and the training of youth were falling into Jewish hands [2C, 10A]. The Jews were seen as turning estates against estates, factions against factions, young against old, individuals against individuals: such fragmentation could only result in chaos and disrespect of established authority. Jewish control over all financial institutions [9C], was seen in the *Protocols* as the necessary requirement for implementing the internationalist designs of the learned elders of Zion [5E].

Little wonder, according to the authors of the pamphlet, that the Jews should preoccupy themselves with the Russian autocracy and the papacy [15A]: these institutions were the strongest bulwarks against liberalism and "western atheism." Antisemites refused to understand the transformation of feudal social relations as the product of either economic class conflict or the quest for freedom on the part of everyday people. They could not consider the collapse of traditional authority as a product of internal problems [18]; it would have meant denying the legitimacy of the very classes and institutions they loved. Works like the *Protocols* instead interpreted the fall of kings and churches as the result of actions by an external enemy and contingent events like assassination or sedition [19]: the antisemite needed his scapegoat.

Antisemites in the past had divorced freedom from equality and all other liberal values. That philosophical move finds an echo in the *Protocols* [4B]. Enlightenment and revolution are seen as products of a successful conspiracy perpetrated by Jews and orchestrated by the learned elders of Zion. The tract highlighted the ability of Jews to flourish in the capitalist economy, play prominent roles in the burgeoning labor movement, and generally dominate the cultural life of the nation. Modernity was understood as the world of the Jews and, if only for this reason, antisemites increasingly fixed their political rage on the "system."

Race became their way of explaining this system and the solidarity of purpose among a seemingly endless array of mutually exclusive interests: bourgeois and proletarian, universal and particular, pacifist and imperialist. The category of race enabled antisemites to fuse this multiplicity into a single enemy. To better realize their purposes, for example, Jews were believed to have created masonic lodges all over the world and seduced the most prominent people into joining them through bribes and propaganda. These lodges, according to the *Protocols,* enabled the elders to organize and centralize their activities [15B]. Its authors insisted that internal discipline was severe and obedience was absolute [15C]: apostates of the cabal supposedly had to be denounced even by members of their own family [17B]. This use of secret masonic lodges by an all-powerful conspiracy of Jews made it possible for the *Protocols* to claim that modernity had been introduced behind the backs of the gentiles and their institutions [11C].

The Jewish conspiracy had apparently existed from time imme-morial, but it was believed to have grown stronger in modern life. All newspapers of all possible political complexions were now controlled by Jews and the *Protocols* put the matter dramatically: "like the Indian idol Vishnu they will have a hundred hands, and every one of them will have a finger on any one of the public opinions as required" [12D]. Even attacks on Jews were believed to have been orchestrated in order to provide the veneer of a liberal society [12B]. All of this was meant to divert good Christians from realizing that the Jews had constituted a "directorate" surrounded by publicists, lawyers, doc-tors, administrators, diplomats, and the like [8A]. Trained in suppos-edly special schools, financed by millionaires, agents of the directorate now permeated every existing organization. Included were even those organizations of a seemingly antisemitic bent since, in that way, the elders of Zion could both manage their "lesser brethren" and foster an illusory belief in freedom of the press [9A]. The inexhaustible power of this new international conspiracy justi-fied the sense of urgency experienced by antisemites in times of crisis even as it provided a built-in explanation for their weakness and any possible strategic mistakes they might make.

It was, of course, the reactionaries rather than the Jews who were engaged in conspiratorial politics. In fact, the last two decades of the nineteenth century were marked by the emergence of new pressure groups like the notoriously antisemitic and imperialist, yet quite respectable, Pan-German League, while in France new political organizational forms appeared in the form of the *Ligue des patriotes* (1883), the *Ligue de la patrie française* (1897) and, the strongest, the *Action Française* (1898). These leagues anticipated the "vanguard party" notion of Lenin with its hierarchy and "cell" structure. The far

right was moving beyond traditional conservatism and experiment-
ing with an explosive mixture of populism, nationalism, and antisemitism. But it seemed to most partisans of the right that the
historical tide was swinging toward the left. This new perspective
indeed became evident in Germany following the elections of 1912,
which became known as "Jewish elections" *(Judenwahlen)*, that
turned the Social Democrats into the largest party in the nation and
resulted in the elimination of the antisemitic political parties as well
as a loss for the traditional right. More than twenty new extraparlia-
mentary antisemitic and ultranationalist organizations came into
existence that would ultimately shape the cultural climate and
political future of the nation in profound ways.[58]

There is a palpable sense of despair in the vision of the future
forwarded by the *Protocols:* modernization appears unstoppable, the
aristocracy is losing its position of preeminence, and the Jews are
apparently sitting in the driver's seat. The Jew is in his element: the
true Christian cannot come to grips with modernity. Works like the
Protocols often mix contempt for the gullibility of the masses with a
grudging respect for the supposedly superior skills of Jews in
manipulating history for their purposes [5B]. The gentiles are "a
flock of sheep": the Jews "are the wolves" [11B]. The antisemite
ultimately engages in a double projection: superior qualities are
superimposed upon an inferior race. Jews understand the nature of
propaganda; they make use of organization; they plot and they plan;
they *know* what political power requires.

Desperation about the future of modernity fueled most early
texts of political antisemitism including the *Protocols.* Its understanding of the Jews, the role they supposedly play and the power they
supposedly hold, differed from what had been presented in the past.
The pamphlet is, for this reason, more than a mere plagiarism of
religious themes or traditional social prejudices. Its view of the Jews
is more encompassing and its understanding of their supposed
planetary ambitions is more radical. Conversion is no longer an
option and it is no longer possible to keep the Jews in their ghettos.
They certainly cannot be citizens like other citizens. There is a cleft
between what they appear to be and what they are. Jews no longer

constitute a visible state within the state, but rather a new and *invisible* society within the society. Given their views, it is not surprising that antisemites should ultimately have launched an international assault against the supposed internal enemies of the national community.

A Universal Alliance of Israelites was organized in 1860 that sought to provide aid for the victims of antisemitic oppression. It sponsored various educational activities and it supported scholarly research projects, but it was never a political force. It could offer little by way of response when its enemies formed an International Antisemitic Congress in 1882 and supported what would become a torrent of hatred against Jews throughout Europe during the next fifteen years: ferocious pogroms in Imperial Russia, trials for ritual crimes in Hungary, the creation of a mass-based antisemitic political party in Austria, an outburst of antisemitic propaganda in Germany, and the riots in the wake of the Dreyfus affair in France.

Zionism was dormant, the quest for a Jewish homeland basically little more than an abstract ideal, when Theodor Herzl called the first Zionist Congress to order in 1897 and began the difficult process of transforming a conglomeration of squabbling sects and organizations into a mass movement. The views of this former assimilationist had changed while covering the Dreyfus affair for an Austrian newspaper.[59] He recognized the injustice of the affair from the very beginning: the only Jew serving on the general staff of the French army, a captain by the name of Alfred Dreyfus, had been accused, convicted, and sent to Devil's Island for selling military secrets to Germany. It gradually became clear, however, that evidence had been doctored, expert witnesses had perjured themselves, due process had been ignored, and a major cover-up had taken place. The real traitor was a dissolute aristocrat, a major in the army, Count Marie-Charles-Ferdinand-Walsin Esterházy.

By the time the affair was finally over, more than a decade later, Dreyfus had been released, a cabinet had been overthrown, and a number of major figures on the general staff had committed suicide. In the meantime, however, the scandal divided France and generated a vicious wave of antisemitism. Herzl concluded that the possibilities for genuine assimilation had vanished: Jews needed their own nation, with its own police and courts, that could serve as a safe haven. But they also needed an organization capable of realizing this goal. Newly energized by the rising tide of anti-Jewish feeling, Herzl sought to unify the Jews as a political force in quest of a Jewish state.

Antisemites were shocked by what their own activities had finally produced. They now sought their own forms of political unity; it indeed seems only logical that the Dreyfus affair should have generated not only Zionism but also the proto-fascist movement, the *Action Française*. This new organizational enterprise called upon antisemites to make sense of their beliefs and the striving of their Jewish enemies in a new way. They would now justify their religious hatreds in secular terms and transform social forms of anti-Judaism into a modern political doctrine of antisemitism. The *Protocols* was an expression of this general undertaking: the political success of the Jewish conspiracy had demanded an unrelenting political response.

The brochure provided a new and even more vigorous distinction between "us" and "them." It unified the Christian interests of otherwise divergent classes, parties, public institutions, and nations. It identified the Jewish conspiracy with *all* the revolutionary trends comprising modernity. It gave a traditional establishmentarian, antimodern, and counterrevolutionary antisemitism an antiestablishmentarian, modern, and revolutionary character. It confronted the supposedly all-pervasive character of Jewish influence with an all-pervasive response. The new antisemitism was concerned with more than either the conformist demands of Christianity or the simple desire to roll back the emancipation of the Jews. It exhibited a new apocalyptic impulse.

Albeit from a markedly reactionary perspective, the *Protocols* reflected the feeling evoked by the marxist theorist Antonio Gramsci when he wrote "the old is dying and the new is not yet born." Perhaps this partially explains the contradictory quality of the pamphlet. Jews are castigated for introducing liberal institutions, which they completely control, and then condemned for planning to abolish these same institutions once they gain power [11A]. Criticism of the gold standard with its anti-inflationary emphasis upon hard currency [20C, D] occurs in the same breath as criticism of government credit institutions and easy credit policies [21]. Public works and progressive forms of taxation are rejected while concerns over unemployment and poverty are manifest [20A]. The supposed Jewish plan to abolish the Christian religion is met with the call to abolish the Jewish religion. Criticism of the abrogation of freedom envisioned by the Jews is met by calls for despotism [12C].

Muddled thinking of this sort permeates the *Protocols*. Again, basically, it is a matter of recognizing some hidden power at work. The existence of an *invisible* Jewish despotism ultimately justifies the institution of a *visible* antisemitic tyranny committed to an assault upon progress and the political heirs of the Enlightenment heritage: the repeal of modernity is possible only with the eradication of the Jewish spirit. The *Protocols* expresses the fear of what Freud called "the return of the repressed." It projects upon Jews the attributes of the antisemite: the antisemite seeks power and, thus, the Jew is consumed by ambition; the antisemite seeks to dominate the public sphere and, thus, the Jew is accused of controlling it; the antisemite seeks to abolish the religion of his enemy and, thus, the Jew is condemned for seeking to abolish all religions other than his own; the antisemite wishes to employ the educational system for his own ends and, thus, the Jew is accused of perverting education; the antisemite joins highly centralized and militaristic organizations, engages in assassinations and the most self-consciously debased forms of propaganda, but the Jew is castigated for such activities. The antisemite is a despot demanding a *Führer* and the destruction of modern liberal society while the Jew, who has a stake in the liberal society, is condemned for imposing despotism in the name of a "supreme lord" chosen by God [23]. Ironically, there is a sense in which Richard Wagner was correct when he called Jews "the evil conscience of the century."

The image of the Jew constructed in the *Protocols* reminds the antisemitic audience of the fears and longings in their own hearts. Contempt for the masses in a burgeoning mass society is the key to the new antisemitic perspective on mass politics in the modern era.

Since only an elite few can really understand the urgency of the situation—given the supposed Jewish control over the press and the public sphere as well as all financial and political institutions—antisemites long for an authoritarian state in which they can press their message without criticism or opposition. The connection between antidemocratic and antisemitic politics occurs from the very onset of modernity. A liberal democracy necessarily hampers the ability of antisemites to deal with the perceived Jewish conspiracy: they must remain content merely with attempting to *persuade* other gentiles of the Jewish threat in the face of criticism by a host of powerful international forces under supposedly Jewish control.

Léon Poliakov perceptively observed in writing that "if ever there was a field where imagination and literary cliches have done all too much harm, it is truly that of anti-Semitic obsessions which have always involved a typical exaggeration of the power the Jews exercised."[60] In this new phase of antisemitism, however, political rage produced more than a "typical exaggeration." With the *Protocols,* antisemitic thought explodes the *spatial* and *temporal* understanding of the Jewish community: national and linguistic divisions collapse; class and status differentiations disappear; divergent customs and even religious observances lose their relevance. Jews in the diaspora have no homeland, no national language; no loyalty except to one another. Once a recognizable entity ensconced in the ghetto, now they are everywhere and nowhere. What appears as their fundamental weakness, according to the *Protocols,* is precisely the source of their strength: the "gift of the dispersion" gives the battle with the Jew a new international or, better, worldwide dimension [11D].

The rootless race was seen as engaged in an attack upon the Christian nation. Jews were believed to have embraced liberal values only to legitimize the "right to hate" and most thought that they employed socialist notions of equality and science to deny the attributes associated with their race. Antisemites responded by linking their prejudice to chauvinism, authoritarianism, and racism. By the beginning of the twentieth century, it was no longer a matter of rejecting the Jew as a Jew *or* of rejecting the Jew as a person. Both forms of hatred came into play: the Jew would have to be *denied as a*

Jew and, precisely for this reason, *also be denied as a person.* Indeed, if this belief would consign antisemitism to the fringes of political life in most of Europe until after World War I, the implications of the *Protocols* were already clear enough: no place exists for the Jew anywhere and, given the nefarious project in which the elders are supposedly engaged, there is no room for mercy.

FOUR

The Tale of a Forgery:
Inventing the *Protocols*

The *Protocols* is the most influential piece of antisemitic propaganda ever created. The tract was inspired by the first Zionist Congress of 1897 in Basel. A year later, when the forgery was undertaken, Imperial Russia experienced an economic crash: the stock market collapsed, two major banks lay in ruins, and millions found themselves unemployed. The Zionist Congress, which brought together Jewish activists intent on securing a homeland for their people, seemed to justify the warnings of a new antisemitic generation concerned with Jewish dominance over financial institutions and an international Jewish conspiracy intent upon wreaking global havoc.[1]

Publication of the *Protocols* was intended as an assault upon an alleged Jewish plan for world conquest whose origins supposedly lay with Solomon as early as 929 BCE. The trademark of this Jewish enterprise was a snake whose head symbolized the initiates and whose body represented the race. Victor Marsden could note in his epilogue to the English edition of the *Protocols* in 1905 how the "serpent of Judah" had slithered and coiled and curled its way around the world bringing only destruction in its wake. A special map in that edition made clear its course. The snake begins its work by undermining Pericles in Greece and Augustus in Rome, moves into Madrid around the time of Charles V in 1552, and then into Paris around 1790 under Louis XVI. It emigrates to England following the fall of Napoleon I, and then to Berlin in the aftermath of the Franco-Prussian War, ultimately to find its new home in St. Petersburg just before the assassination of Alexander III in 1881. Little wonder that, as a reminder, most editions of the *Protocols* present a snake or an octopus coiling around a globe on the cover.

The idea of an ubiquitous secret society, alien and evil, supernaturally powerful and sexually corrupt, intent upon dominating the world has its roots in the Roman Empire. Pagans saw a conspiracy of this sort being perpetrated by Christians and, later, Christians would identify various cabals of heretics, Jews, and witches.[2] The sources of conspiracy are numerous and often esoteric. There were the famous soldiers known as the Templars, whose order was dissolved in 1314, but whose activity was said to continue down into modernity. There was the brotherhood of the Rosicrucians with their manifesto of 1615, whose authors still remain unknown but whose power was supposedly enormous. Of particular concern for advocates of the *Protocols,* however, were the Freemasons.[3]

The term derives from England in the eleventh century when groups of "free masons," who did not belong to any local guild of brick-layers, traveled from place to place along with artists, builders, and architects plying their trade and searching for large-scale projects like the construction of churches. Organized in what would come to be known as "lodges," or the log houses originally used as workstations and meeting rooms, the Freemasons were an exclusive group and therefore gave rise to much speculation. In the eighteenth century, they opened their doors to people with different interests and occupations. The first German lodge was founded in 1737 in Hamburg and, in the following year, the Prussian Crown Prince, who would later become Frederick the Great, became a member. But this did nothing to quell popular suspicions. The Freemasons were criticized for being what later reactionaries liked to call "rootless" and also for their tolerance. Constantly under threat of repression by the church and often secular authorities, it made sense for the Freemasons to meet in secret. As a consequence of this no less than their international character and their nondenominational views, they soon became known as a conspiratorial sect. Indeed, because they employed secret signals and ensignia, its members were believed to "know one another without having seen one another."

According to their critics, the Freemasons were organized in strict hierarchical fashion. Disobedience to a Grand Master was supposedly punishable by death; this provided their critics a built-in explanation for every inexplicable assassination committed anywhere in the world.[4] Tightly knit and secular in orientation, identified with liberal intellectual and artistic pursuits, the Freemasons, it was believed, were engaged in a secret war against the monarchy and the papacy. Voltaire, Turgot, Condorcet, Diderot, and d'Alembert were considered their agents and from this circle, according to this reactionary ideology, came the Jacobins. Apparently, however, the Jacobins had many masters since they were also supposedly controlled by an even more radical ally of the Freemasons, known as the Illuminati, who were grounded in Bavaria and obsessed with regicide and the assassination of royalty.[5] It apparently mattered little that the Illuminati, about whom relatively little is known, were rivals of the Freemasons and that the sect was officially dissolved in 1786, three years before the outbreak of the French Revolution.

The mostly forgotten Abbé Barruel in his multivolume *Memoirs in the Service of the Revolution* castigated these groups. He considered them the real instigators of the French Revolution until he received a letter from the now totally forgotten J. B. Simonini, itself a possible forgery committed by the legendary police chief Fouché. The letter informed him that the Freemasons and the Illuminati were both founded by Jews, that hundreds of the highest ecclesiastics were Jews, and that the "accursed race" had poisoned any number of monarchs over the centuries. Its leaders had apparently underwritten the writings of the Enlightenment *philosophes,* dominated the Jacobins, and were now intent on world conquest. The Jews and the Freemasons, in this way, became linked with the *philosophes* in the paranoid imagination of reactionaries; it has even been suggested that the alliance between them was secured through a contract between the Freemasons and the B'nai B'rith after its founding in 1843.[6]

None of these groups, of course, were particularly interested in the Jews.[7] There was nothing secret about the *philosophes,* Jews had no interaction with the Illuminati, and few Jews participated in the masonic lodges of the Freemasons. But the feudal past carried over into the modern era. The perverse images of "the Jew" and the mistaken beliefs regarding the "Christ-killers" had an impact: it is not surprising that, since the beginning of the eighteenth century, Jews should have been seen as dominating an all-encompassing conspiracy directed against Christian civilization.

In Russia, where antisemitism was officially sponsored, Jacob Brafmann introduced the legend of a conspiracy through his two books, *The Local and Universal Jewish Brotherhoods* (1868) and *The Book of the Kahal* (1869). This "Jewish expert" for the governor general of the Northwest region of Russia saw the *kahal,* a form of self-government, as part of a vast network controlled by the Universal Alliance of Israelites. This network was purportedly concerned with undermining Christian entrepreneurs, taking over all their property, and ultimately seizing political power. It is indeed tempting to engage in a genealogical analysis of the supposed Jewish cabal against Christian civilization. The stories can prove riotously funny. In France, for example, they:

> . . . appealed above all to the country clergy—nearly all of them sons of peasants or of village artisans, poorly educated, infinitely credulous. What they were prepared to believe beggars description. In 1893 that great hoaxer, Leo Taxil, had no difficulty at all in persuading them that the head of American Freemasonry had a telephone system invented and manned (if that is the word) by devils, and so was kept in constant touch with the seven major capitals of the world; or that beneath the Rock of Gibralter squads of devils were at work, concocting epidemics to destroy the Catholic world. And if Taxil confines his attention to Freemasons and makes no mention of Jews, others were less restrained.[8]

The idea of a Jewish conspiracy, however, gained currency not simply because of outlandish nonsense of this sort. *The Book of the*

Kahal was printed at public expense, circulated among numerous officials, and treated as a serious text for governmental agents.[9] It gave the Jewish threat an international dimension and linked it with the nationalities problem, a link that would survive and play a role in Russian history down to the present. The idea of a Jewish conspiracy also fit nicely with a broader conservative political philosophy of restoration, obsessed with the ways in which the "crowd" and the "mass" were being misled by the new critical spirit of modernity. The French Revolution undertaken against a monarchy rooted in ancient traditions—if not according to Edmund Burke or Alexis de Tocqueville, then according to those far more extreme in their conservative views—could *only* have been the work of an outsider or Antichrist intent on deceiving the French people; only the Freemason or the Jew, or most likely both, could possibly have fomented a cataclysm of such proportions.

THE *PROTOCOLS* FIND A HOME

This antisemitic attitude was international in its influence. But nowhere was it more influential than in Russia. This nation was not only the most economically underdeveloped among what were known as "the great powers," but was also perhaps the most politically and culturally retrograde. Despite its glittering literary tradition which included giants like Pushkin, Dostoyevsky, and Tolstoy, who illuminated the problems of the nation with striking clarity, its culture was generally suspicious of liberal ideals and western individualism. Imperial Russia was dominated by an insular court and a medieval orthodox church. Its oddly messianic nationalism helped generate the first pogroms in modern Europe, and its theocratic political structure rendered the state inflexible and closed to any ideas of reform. Its disparities of wealth, its contrasts between a few large cities and a vast impoverished countryside, its mass illiteracy and religious obscurantism, its absolutism and lack of a genuine public sphere made it a perfect setting for the publication of the *Protocols* when it first appeared in 1903. The pamphlet would serve as the clarion call for the pogrom in Kishinev, Bessarabia, which would leave forty-five Jews dead.

The vehicle for its publication was *The Banner (Znamya)*, a newspaper in St. Petersburg published by a well-known antisemite, P. A. Krushevan, who was among the principal instigators. He and his friend G. V. Butmi, who would later publish a second variant entitled *The Root of Our Troubles,* were both members of the True Friends of the Russian People, an extremely crude antisemitic group popularly known as the Black Hundreds. Organized during the reign of Czar Alexander III, this group anticipated Mussolini's Black Shirts and the notorious S.A. or Brown Shirts of the Nazis. It had support among certain aristocrats and high government bureaucrats. Especially in the cities, however, criminals and ruffians predominated in the Black Hundreds. This organization would turn the *Protocols* into its manifesto.

Sergei Nilus first included the text in 1905 as an appendix to the second edition of his 1903 book entitled *The Great in the Small: The Coming of the Anti-Christ and the Rule of Satan on Earth,* which tells of his conversion from a worldly intellectual into a religious mystic. He republished it again in an expanded edition in 1917 entitled *It Is Near at Our Doors!* warning of a coming apocalypse initiated by the Jews. Knowledge about the life of Sergei Nilus is even more sketchy than knowledge about the origins of the *Protocols.* The best source derives from a young man, Armand Alexandre du Chayla,[10] who was engaged in religious research during the beginning of the early twentieth century. Traveling around Russia, Chayla made his way to the famous cloister known as Optina Poustine. It had been visited by numerous writers, and Dostoyevsky used one of its elders as a model for Father Zossima in *The Brothers Karamazov.* There Chayla encountered Nilus, who, having returned to the area after failed careers as a businessman, a landowner, and a judge, lived nearby with his wife, Jelenea Alexandrowna Oserowa, and his former mistress, Natalya Komarovskaya.[11]

The son of Swiss émigrés who had entered Russia during the reign of Peter I, Nilus boasted of being a direct descendant of a special executioner under Ivan the Terrible. A mystic and a crank, well educated and intensely reactionary, eccentric and easily slighted, he apparently spoke perfect French and admired the critique of civilization developed by Nietzsche. Jailed by the Bolsheviks, later a nomadic wanderer, he would die peacefully of heart failure on January 14, 1929 at the age of sixty-seven. The apples did not fall far from the tree: his son would offer his services to the Nazis and his beloved niece would work for numerous antisemitic organizations in France, Germany, and the United States until her death in 1989 at the age of 96.[12]

Chayla and his new friend immediately began talking about religious issues and, soon enough, Nilus offered to show him an explosive document. Chayla began to read the *Protocols:* he knew right away that it was not the work of a French native, given the numerous idiomatic and spelling mistakes, and he also noted three different inks and three different styles of handwriting in what was a small notebook with a blue ink stain. But Nilus sought to counter his skepticism. The proof for the grand plan harbored by the Jewish conspiracy, which he would later emphasize in the 1911 edition of the *Protocols,* rested on the existence of various objects ranging from household utensils to certain school insignia to the cross of the Legion of Honor, in which he perceived a triangle or a pair of crossed triangles or, what he considered, "the seal of the Antichrist."

Paranoia has always been an element of antisemitism and Nilus was a case in point. He saw the Jew everywhere; 1911 would find him addressing a letter to the Patriarchs of the Orient, to the Holy Synod, and to the Pope calling upon them to ally in order to protect Christianity against the Antichrist. Every Jew he encountered was a threat. Nilus even refused to keep his copy of the *Protocols* in his own house, leaving it instead with a friend, for fear of agents like the Jewish druggist who once mistakenly crossed his lawn. Nilus was obsessed. It was the same with his friends and other publishers of the *Protocols.* They were never really concerned with its authenticity. Nilus made the point clearly enough: "When I first became acquainted with the contents of the manuscript I was convinced that its terrible truth is witness of its true origin from the 'Zionist men of Wisdom' and that no other evidence of its origin would be needed."[13]

ORIGINS

Many are the versions of how the *Protocols* originated.[14] Some claimed it was initially written in Hebrew and translated by Nilus, who was often falsely presented as a professor of oriental languages, while others argued the author of the work was an alienated Jew. Some suggested the pamphlet was the minutes of the Basel congress, and others that it was handed down from generation to generation. Some claimed that its authors were the Elders of Zion, who were identical with the Zionists led by Herzl, while others believed that the *Protocols* was written by Asher Ginsberg, whose pseudonym was Ahad Ha'am, for a secret organization known as the Sons of Moses.[15] No verification was, needless to say, ever provided for any of these views by anyone who accepted the pamphlet as genuine.[16]

Critics of the *Protocols* made their case following its translation into English as *The Jewish Peril* in 1920. Princess Katarina Radziwill essentially confirmed Chayla's account in an interview from her exile in 1921 for *American Hebrew* and, after much arm-twisting, her arch-reactionary and antisemitic girlfriend Henriette Harblut also supported the story. Both were popular at court in their youth, privy to many secrets and close friends with officials of the *Okhrana*. They apparently saw the same notebook with the blue ink spot and Princess Radziwill seems to have heard her contact in the secret police, Golinsky, speak about the forgery and an international Jewish conspiracy. Both considered the *Protocols* merely a tool to stir up the Cossacks and the Black Hundreds against the Jews; they maintained that the pamphlet was not taken seriously by anyone of substance at the Imperial Court.[17] Finally, also in 1921, Philip Graves learned from an informant named Raslovlev, who had seen the original manuscript, that the *Protocols* was a distorted plagiarism of *A Dialogue in Hell* by Maurice Joly.[18]

Antisemitic tales concerning the discovery of the *Protocols* proved far more imaginative. Krushevan probably took the most intelligent approach: undoubtedly fearful of endangering his friends, he simply refused to reveal how he obtained the manuscript from the "Central Chancellory of Zion in France." His friend, Butmi, by contrast claimed that it was smuggled out from Zionist "secret archives," which it would be impossible to reenter, and translated page by page from French into German. Gottfried zur Beek, who later edited the first German edition of the *Protocols,* insisted the Elders of Zion were betrayed by a Jew entrusted with taking the minutes of the Basel Congress; it seems that, for an unspecified bribe, he had secured safety in an unnamed town for an unnamed spy for the Russian government, who had with him a number of unnamed copyists. Still others have suggested that a Jewish member of the Freemasons by the name of Joseph Host—alias Shapiro—sold the *Protocols* in a daring undercover operation to Madame Justine Glinka,[19] daughter of a Russian general, who translated the work and passed it along to Alexis Sukhotin: once, as vice governor of Sebastopol, he had an entire peasant village arrested for refusing to carry infected manure from his stables to his fields.[20] Later editions of the work, however, would frame the matter in yet another way:

> The origins of the Protocols are shrouded in the deepest darkness. The Protocols itself present a series of speeches, which occurred among a larger circle of listeners. When and where this took place, who wrote up and first presented them to the public, all this is no longer possible to ascertain. Many are the rumors concerning the origins of the Protocols. . . . The Jews have used the darkness surrounding the origins of the Protocols to present them as a forgery. Nevertheless, the inexplainable origins of the Protocols actually speak more for their authenticity than against it; it is clear, after all, that such a dangerous and secret document could only have been brought to light by the darkest means.[21]

As for the main character in the drama, Sergei Nilus, he provided different versions of how he had acquired the *Protocols* in different editions of the work. If his fragmentary remembrances were to be pieced together into something resembling a coherent account, it would read thus: Nilus received a notebook containing the minutes of the secret Basel congress from his friend, Sukhotin, who had obtained it in 1902 from an anonymous woman. She had secretly copied it with two friends after discovering the *Protocols* in a closet, which also contained the "archives of the Central Chancellory of Zion," while spending a night with one of the "most influential" leaders of Jewish Freemasonry; the man in question had apparently been called away on business. Chayla would later claim that the woman was really none other than Natalya Komarovskaya, the mistress of Nilus. But this was never proven. Neither Nilus nor his mistress ever gave the high official of Zionism a name, disclosed the location of the apartment, or explained what the other copiers, who also remained anonymous, were doing there. It is also somewhat difficult to understand why a vast conspiracy like that of the Elders of Zion should have kept their most valuable documents in a closet.

Other problems emerge from the account offered by Nilus. He could not make up his mind whether the *Protocols* were procured from Paris or Switzerland. Also, although the Zionist Congress at Basel took place in 1897, Nilus insisted the "minutes" were taken from an unspecified and historically undocumented meeting in 1902. Then, too, it makes little sense that the minutes should have originally been taken in French since the Basel congress was conducted in German and not a single French delegate was present. Members of the "society" who supposedly signed the document were never identified: it also seems that when Nilus identified the elders as the "Zionist representatives of the 33rd Degree in Oriental Freemasonry," he unwittingly transferred the use of "degrees" from Freemasonry to Zionism. But, then, Nilus had an answer for everything. Indeed, when asked by Chayla whether he believed in the authenticity of the pamphlet, the mystic apparently replied: "Did not the ass of Balaam utter prophecy? Cannot God transform the bones of a dog into sacred miracles? If he can do these things, he can also make the announcement of truth come from the mouth of a liar."[22]

SOURCES

The *Protocols* were probably forged sometime between 1894 and 1899. These years marked the high point of the Dreyfus affair. It was a time when markedly similar claims to those articulated in the

Protocols were being argued in any number of popular magazines, including the infamous daily *La Libre parole* edited by Edouard Drumont, and in what would become modern classics of antisemitism: *The Jew, Judaism, and the Jewification of the Christian People* (1869) by Gougenot des Mousseaux, *World Conquest by the Jews* (1870) by Osman-Bey, *The Talmud and the Jews* (1879-80) by Hippolytus Lutostansky, *The Jewish Question as a Racial, Moral, and Cultural Question* by Eugen Dühring (1881), *Jewish France* (1886) by Drumont, and *The Foundations of the Nineteenth Century* (1899) by Houston Stewart Chamberlain.

These books were primarily historical or philosophical works. And many were best-sellers or sold exceptionally well. Indeed, antisemitism has its own literary tradition. The first literary work in which a Jewish conspiracy against Christian society figured as the prominent theme was probably "The Undivine Comedy" by an early nineteenth-century, romantic and nationalist, Polish poet, named Zygmont Krasinski. The theoretical extravagances of the pseudophilosophers and pseudohistorians were given dramatic form in works like these and nowhere more so than in a particularly malevolent novel of 1868 entitled *Biarritz*. Supposedly written by Sir John Retcliffe, it would help forge the myth of the *Protocols*. The real author was a former employee in the Prussian postal service named Hermann Goedsche (1815-78). He had been dismissed from his job for forging documents to discredit Benedict Waldeck, an important democratic politician, in the aftermath of the German Revolution of 1848. Soon after, Goedsche became an informer, agent, and spy for the government. He published several works in the form of memoirs and historical romances under the pseudonym Sir John Retcliffe and, especially in Imperial Russia, his works became remarkably well known.

Gothic in form and semipornographic in content, Goedsche's novels were mass market thrillers. The style had gained a certain vogue through the writings of Alexandre Dumas and *The Mysteries of Paris* by Eugene Sue,[23] which Karl Marx particularly enjoyed, but the infusion of antisemitic images and ideas into the form was the contribution of Goedsche. A chapter from *Biarritz* (1868) would indeed presage the *Protocols*.[24] It takes place at the Jewish cemetery in

Prague and it describes a supposed gathering of the elect, or the "elders," from the twelve tribes of the Jews—though ten had in reality been lost to history. The meeting is dominated by the speech of a single individual: the leading elder, or Chief Rabbi, of the Jews and the architect of their plans for world conquest.[25]

The melodrama proceeds slowly. The cemetery is pitch-black and silent. Each representative from the "Elect of Israel" moves through the cemetery in a ghostlike fashion until he reaches the tomb of "a Holy Rabbi, Simeon ben Jehudah," upon which he kneels, bends his head three times, and offers a prayer. When they are finally all assembled, when the chief rabbi finally appears and takes his place as the thirteenth personage, a loud sound is heard and the devil greets them. The meeting begins at midnight. Strategies are debated, and each of the elders reports on his activities. Various attempts are described to manipulate the stock exchange, deepen national debts, seize land, control newspapers, dominate political parties, form a proletariat, destroy the church, subvert the military, instigate international conflict, institute civil liberties, legalize intermarriage.

"No century is better suited for our success than this one," says a participant, "the future is ours!"[26] The others agree. Each tosses a stone on the tomb and a "huge gold shapeless figure of an animal," undoubtedly the golden calf, appears. They are then bid adieu. The Jews disperse, happy in anticipation of the next meeting of their grandsons one hundred years hence. Unfortunately for them, though luckily for the future of Christendom, the Jews are unaware that they are being observed by a German scholar and a baptized Jew, whose fears and disgust generate a radical commitment to struggle against this fiendish conspiracy.

The scene at the Jewish Cemetery in Prague depicted in *Biarritz* made the fictional conspiracy seem real; it had a huge impact. A literal translation of the chapter into Russian appeared in St. Petersburg in 1872 and in 1876 in Moscow, followed by a second edition in 1880. In July of 1881, the crucial chapter appeared in the French journal *Le Contemporain* having been fashioned into a seemingly authentic speech that would become commonly known as "The Rabbi's Speech."[27] It then appeared in the *Catechism for*

Antisemites by Theodor Fritsch that would later be expanded into the *Handbook on the Jewish Question* whose sales reached 100,000 when he died in 1933. In the same year, 1887, the chapter appeared again in France in the antisemitic anthology entitled *La Russe juive* and, in 1893, it was published in the Austrian review, *Deutsch-sozialen Blätter*. In 1901, the speech was translated into the Czech language, but it was confiscated by the authorities. When the Czech parliamentary deputy Brzenovski read the speech to the Reichstag in Vienna as an interpellation, however, it was immediately published in two other Austrian papers. In 1903, of course, Kruschevan would employ it to inflate the Bessarabian pogroms of that year and, in 1906, his friend Butmi included it in his publication of the *Protocols*.

This "Rabbi's Speech" transformed a work of fiction into a supposed statement of fact: the cemetery scene described in *Biarritz* was thereby given a new ring of truth.[28] Even intelligent people like the noted historian Heinrich von Treitschke took the fiction for reality. The speech would often, moreover, become confused with the larger tract. And, in a certain sense, it can be seen as a type of capsule version. Ludwig Müller who published the *Protocols* in 1919 under the pseudonym Gottfried zur Beek even included the speech in the introduction to his German edition of the work as collateral proof of a Jewish conspiracy.[29] It is true that the connection between the speech and *Biarritz* was already known by that time and that an exhaustive comparison of the novel and the *Protocols* had been completed in 1920.[30] Nevertheless, the harm had already been done.

If *Biarritz* served as the basis for "The Rabbi's Speech," however, a work of a very different character and quality served as the basis for the *Protocols*. It is indeed ironic that *A Dialogue in Hell: Conversations Between Machiavelli and Montesquieu about Power and Right,* written by Maurice Joly, should initially have been intended as a defense of republicanism and a critique of the authoritarianism instituted by Napoleon III. The plagiarizers used more than 160 paragraphs from this obscure work, more than half of 9 different chapters, and even ordered most of them in the same way. The irony of employing a liberal work of this kind for reactionary purposes is striking. But choosing this work to plagiarize wasn't completely insane. Both Joly and his *Dialogue* had been completely forgotten at the time the *Protocols* was composed.

Written in 1864, when Joly was thirty-one, the *Dialogue* was initially published in Belgium in order to avoid the censors and smuggled into France. But the ruse didn't work; Joly soon found himself arrested. Fifteen months later he was released and he occupied his time writing novels and various polemics. After initially welcoming the Paris Commune of 1871, he was arrested once again on trumped up charges of libel and treason. The fall of the Commune and the creation of the Third Republic didn't change his luck. Unsuccessful in his literary pursuits, sick, and bitter, he committed suicide in 1879, long before his work would be cynically employed by those whom he would have despised. Indeed, by putting the words of Joly's fictional Machiavelli into the mouth of an equally fictional Jewish elder, an antisemitic tract of immense importance was born.

Antisemitic advocates of the *Protocols* would later become intent upon proving that Maurice Joly was actually a Jew named Moishe Joel, who had fallen under the influence of Adolphe Isaac Cremieux, the founder of the Universal Alliance of Israelites.[31] Others, including more modern authors sharply critical of antisemitism, would underscore his supposed connection with the Freemasons.[32] Still others would suggest that it was not really the authors of the *Protocols* who plagiarized Joly, but Joly who had plagiarized another Jew named Jacob Venedey, who in 1847 supposedly helped Marx found the secret Communist League, which, they claimed, was an offshoot of the Society for Jewish Culture and Science (*Verein für Kunst und Wissenschaft der Juden*).[33] Thus, according to antisemites, the source of the *Protocols* was two Jews if not Cremieux himself, and its connection with marxism, the inspiration for socialism and communism, occurred from its inception.

Marx and Engels were indeed leaders of the London-based Communist League (*Bund der Kommunisten*), formerly the League of the Just (*Bund der Gerechten*), from 1847 until its dissolution in 1852. This secret league of German intellectuals and craftsmen in exile called upon them to write its statute or program, which later became known as *The*

Communist Manifesto. These organizations of the early labor movement, however, had nothing to do with the Society for Jewish Culture and Science that existed from 1819-1824. Marx also never worked with Venedey, and Joly was not a Jew (his parents were Italian and Catholic). Why the Chief Elder of Zion should not have mentioned his source to his Jewish audience, given the degree to which his speech relies upon the work of Joly, is also somewhat difficult to understand. Even if Joly were a Jew or a Freemason, antisemitic interpretations avoid dealing with his support for Montesquieu and republicanism rather than, as outlined in the *Protocols,* Machiavelli and his plans for an authoritarian state. The plagiarism of Joly's work clearly involved a perversion of its political intent.

The question remains how a group of Russian agents, not particularly well versed in French political literature, discovered Joly's work. Connections between reactionary circles in France and Russia had been strong since Joseph de Maistre served as the French Ambassador to Moscow in the middle of the nineteenth century. And they only became stronger as the fear of an international Jewish conspiracy increased during the early 1880s. Antisemitic members of the Russian aristocracy frequented the salon of Juliette Adam whose participants included Edouard Drumont and the consultant for his enormously popular antisemitic magazine, *La Libre parole,* Count Esterházy previously mentioned as the guilty party in the Dreyfus affair. It was most likely in this salon or from a figure like Drumont that Russian antisemites visiting France should have learned of the work by Maurice Joly.[34]

The plagiarism of the *Protocols* from the *Dialogue* itself is indisputable. The general structural similarity of both works is striking. Protocols 1-19 generally correspond with Dialogues 1-17; only the next five protocols, except for a few paraphrases, have anything original about them. The last sections describe the success of the enterprise when the House of David finally rules the world and a messianic age dawns. There was little the forgers of the *Protocols* could garner from the remaining dialogues since they dealt almost exclusively with issues pertaining to the second empire of Napoleon III. Comparisons of the texts were already made in the 1920s and they have been reprinted often.[35] There are certain problems given the many different versions of the *Protocols* and supporters of the pamphlet have been quick to note minor inconsistencies. Nevertheless, two brief examples of the way that the *Dialogue* was employed in the widely circulated German edition of the *Protocols* published by Gottfried zur Beek should make the point

> *Dialogue*: Government by the people destroys all stability and sanctifies an undefined right of revolution. It plunges society into an open battle against all the powers of the divine and human world order. It transforms the people into a beast of prey that is not satisfied until it has tasted blood. (Joly, p. 35).

> *Protocols*: The word liberty plunges human society into a struggle against all powers, against every divine and natural part of the world order. As soon as we sit upon the throne, we shall strike this word from the vocabulary of mankind because it is at the heart of that bestial power which reduces the masses to the level of the beast of prey. Only after they have tasted blood are they satisfied. (zur Beek, p. 83)

> *Dialogue*: Like the God Vishnu, my press will have a hundred arms, each hand of which will feel the nuances of public opinion. (Joly, p. 106)

> *Protocols*: Like the Indian pagan god Vishnu, they will have one hundred hands, and in each shall beat the pulse of a different intellectual tendency. (zur Beek, p. 104).[36]

Joly's imaginary conversation between two giants of political theory on the future of democracy is an admirable work and quite salient in its insights on the nature of modern government and the possibilities attendant upon the arbitrary exercise of power. Machiavelli is clearly the central figure and he is interpreted in terms common to the nineteenth century when the "great man" theory of Thomas Carlyle was dominant and nation-building was understood as the primary task in continental Europe. The Italian thinker appears as a proponent of *raison d'état* and a unitary state led by a dictator whose fundamental concern is maintaining power and dividing his enemies through a combination of propaganda and terror. Machiavelli does most of the talking and, only in the first six of the twenty-four dialogues, does Montesquieu really respond in more than exclamatory terms. Liberty leads only to anarchy for the chief elder of the *Protocols* and the Machiavelli of the *Dialogue*. Both are intent on controlling the press and both identify political resistance with criminality purely and simply. Parliamentary organs are meant only for manipulation, a police state is the source of power, and the leader must appear moral even if he acts only in his own interests. Power has nothing to do with morality; it is its own justification.

Joly condemned the tactics and the vision of Machiavelli, which the *Protocols* would attribute to the Jews, through the towering figure of Montesquieu. His political theory, with its commitment to Enlightenment values, is used by Joly to contest the despotism of Napoleon III. The more aristocratic elements in the thinking of Montesquieu never appear in the portrait by Joly. Montesquieu is instead depicted as an uncritical representative of republicanism committed to the accountability of government, written constitutions, and the separation of powers. The prophetic element in the *Dialogue,* however, is the weakness of Joly's own republican position in countering authoritarian arguments: its programmatic vacuum is apparent along with its seemingly naive reliance on ethical values, and its trust in the masses. Egoism is on the verge of overpowering reason and instrumental realism is intent on abolishing norms. Indeed, whatever its influence on the *Protocols,*[37] the genuinely anticipatory character of the *Dialogue* derives more from its generally dark vision concerning the prospects for authoritarianism than its actual understanding of modern totalitarianism.

Joly never imagined the ways that ideological motivations would inform totalitarian movements and the quest for political power. He had no sense of the extent to which it would be possible to create and implement a cult of the personality in a very new form of the bureaucratic state. He also could not have conceived mass murder taking place for its own sake rather than as a form of purposive action. Napoleon III was not Hitler. That is why the *Dialogue*, whatever the incredible extent to which it was plagiarized, would ultimately prove insufficient for the forgers of the *Protocols*.

Machiavelli does not simply turn into the rabbi. The words are the same, but the rabbi is a very different character. His realism is infused with a far more sinister purpose; his power is no longer employed for the purpose of maintaining itself, or even of simply dominating the world, but of destroying Christian civilization and instituting a qualitatively new utopian—or disutopian—order. *Biarritz* was an essential supplement to the *Dialogue*. It would provide instrumental realism with an infusion of principle, so to speak, and the new purely mythical context in which it could prove operative. In short, the *Protocols* would rely on both works though in very different ways.

COURT INTRIGUES

The *Protocols* were most likely procured by Nilus from the director of the foreign branch of the Russian secret police named Piotor Rachovsky, who was less concerned with ideology than his own advancement.[38] He would certainly have been the right man for the job. While in France, under the pseudonym Jean Préval, Rachovsky had written a work entitled *Anarchism and Nihilism* (1892) that contained many of the themes dealt with in the *Protocols*. He had also forged a host of other documents in his years spent infiltrating and discrediting the various dissident circles of Russians living abroad. It seems that Rachovsky had burglarized the home of a certain Elie de Cyon under the orders of his boss, the famous minister of finance Sergei Witte. Cyon had been an adamant critic of the modernization program initiated by Witte. Its emphasis on increased production in the industrial sector coupled with an introduction of the gold standard posed an obvious threat to the economic primacy of the landed aristocracy and its traditional values. Cyon is often seen as the author of the *Protocols,* but that is highly doubtful. He was a converted Jew without evident antisemitic biases, a physiologist and a political commentator, and an intellectual. It is unlikely that de Cyon would have forged a crude document like the *Protocols,* laden with grammatical and spelling mistakes. He apparently knew of Joly's work, however, and used it in creating a satire of his own. This was probably used, in turn, by Rachovsky's agents in creating the tract. Most likely, "Joly's satire on Napoleon III was transformed by de Cyon into a satire on Witte which was then transformed under Rachovsky's guidance into *The Protocols of the Elders of Zion.*"[39]

The pamphlet expresses fear about the growing influence of socialism upon Jewish organizations in Russia. It also evidences concern over the rise of the staunchly anti-Zionist and secularist Jewish Bund with its tripartite commitment to republicanism, socialism, and the rights of national cultural autonomy for Jews in the Russian diaspora. Jews had gained a certain measure of autonomy inside the infamous Pale of Settlement, the western territory where they had been concentrated since the end of the eighteenth century, and the czar feared the power of a non-Russian nationality which did not have a historic right to self-rule.[40] Jews seeking national self-determination for their people might well cause problems with other groups and also set a precedent for other stronger minorities like the Poles, Belorussians, Lithuanians, and Ukrainians.[41]

The times were fortuitous for the pamphlet. What has been termed a "permanent pogrom against Russian Jews" was initiated in 1882 following the assassination of Alexander II and it continued into the aftermath of the Revolution of 1905.[42] This led to the creation of armed Jewish self-defense squads fostered by political organizations like the Bund. The year 1905 marked the high point of the Russo-Japanese War and the culmination of a revolutionary wave of strikes, which had begun in Baku in 1902 and gradually reached St. Petersburg, where a democratic "soviet" of more than 140,000 people was constituted. A conscious policy of Jew-baiting followed the defeat of Russia by Japan on the battlefield and the disaster for the aristocracy brought about by the Revolution of 1905.

Judeophobia was, in short, an important part of the political climate when the *Protocols* first appeared and the pamphlet would ultimately play an important part in a court intrigue with extraordinary implications. It was initially intended by the double-dealing Rachovsky to discredit Sergei Witte. As chief Russian plenipotentiary, he had worked hard for the treaty signed at the Portsmouth Peace Conference and he also virtually forced the czar to grant a constitution. The imperial court hated him and the czar referred to his circle as "the Jewish clique." Witte was nearly killed by the Black Hundreds, and two Jewish members of the Duma, Yollos and Hertzenstein, were actually assassinated.[43] His liberal program of industrialization was popularly identified with the interests of Jews and Freemasons; it was indeed seen as part of a more general conspiratorial attempt to undermine the traditions of the Russian empire.

Enter Sergei Nilus. The mystic liked to present himself as an otherworldly saint. But this liar was also a man of ambition. *The Great in the Small* had impressed the Grand Duchess Elisabeth Fiodorovna and she, an avowed reactionary, believed its author would serve as a good influence on the czar.[44] His book seemed to justify the fears inspired by the Universal Alliance of Israelites and the Jewish self-defense squads in Russia. The *Protocols* simultaneously identified democracy with Jewish interests and enabled the populace to believe there was something worse than existing forms of authoritarianism. The extreme nationalism of the pamphlet, combined with its hatred of republicanism and socialism, indeed fit perfectly with the ideology of the most conservative court faction and its principal advocate, the Grand Duchess Elisabeth.

Her opposition to western notions of modernity and France, birthplace of the Enlightenment, was implacable; it was no different with the leading political representative of her faction, the vicious antisemite and future minister of the interior V. K. Plehve, who was the arch-enemy of Witte. This faction was committed to reversing the various reforms achieved during the Revolution of 1905, and especially those affecting the freedom of the Jews. That also meant undermining the relatively liberal influence of a certain Philippe, a faith healer and mystic from Lyons, who was serving as the religious counselor to the czar and czarina, and who always began his seances with Nicholas and Alexandra and their ancestors with the cry, *Vive la France!*[45]

Nilus may well have spent much of this time absent from Moscow and in religious seclusion. But his work became known to the grand duchess and the conservative opposition at court. Gottfried zur Beek would later declare that Nilus had been an employee of the secret police.[46] But, whether or not this was actually the case, he knew Rachovsky and it seems likely that one extreme reactionary should have sought to help another—and perhaps himself—by placing in his possession a document of such importance. The first copy of the *Protocols* was given to the czar. He was delighted. His marginal notes included statements like "What depth of thought!," "How prophetic!," "How perfectly they have fulfilled their plan!," "This year of 1905 has truly been dominated by the Jewish Elders," "All of it is undoubtedly genuine! The destructive hand of Jewry is everywhere!"

Philippe fell from power: the last straw was when he convinced the czarina that she would become pregnant with a male heir and she then suffered a false pregnancy that made her the laughingstock of Europe.[47] The Grand Duchess Elisabeth recognized what had *really* taken place: the czar and czarina had obviously been duped by a Freemason from France, an accomplice of world Jewry, whose leaders had caused chaos by calling in the Japanese to destroy Holy Russia. She counseled the royal couple to replace him with a genuine Russian and a true reactionary. The author of *The Great in the Small* seemed poised for victory; arrangements were made for his formal entry into the priesthood and he even ordered priestly clothes.

Unfortunately, however, the supporters of Philippe took their revenge. They conspired to prevent the entry of Nilus into the clergy by publicizing a scandal about his mistress. Though Philippe soon enough lost his influence at court and returned to France and obscurity, once again, the mystic found himself ruined. He wandered from monastery to monastery until his wife was finally granted a pension by the czar in 1905, which made it possible for Nilus to publish a second edition of his 1903 work. Meanwhile, at the imperial court, intrigue continued over who would serve as the next religious counselor for the royal couple. With their usual unerring accuracy and insight into the needs of their nation, they chose a psychotic of independent spirit: Rasputin.

Enough sentiment and misplaced nostalgia have been expended on behalf of Nicholas and Alexandra and their court.[48] The royal couple and much of their entourage would, of course, meet a brutal end at the hands of the Bolsheviks. But they were representative of the worst in a traditional order whose virtues have been vastly exaggerated. Nicholas and Alexandra were enemies of everything connected with the liberal legacy of the Enlightenment. They encouraged, usually from behind the scenes, the Black Hundreds and their pogroms and, in subsequent years, pardoned virtually everyone convicted of being involved in those atrocities.[49] Maurice Samuel was indeed correct when he called these refined monarchs "bloodthirsty by proxy." They lacked even a hint of knowledge about foreign affairs, modern economics, or the social trends at work in their empire. Without the least empathy for the miserable lives led by their subjects, both were pathetically arrogant, politically reactionary, close-minded autocrats of weak character, and ill-equipped to rule.

They initially embraced the *Protocols* enthusiastically; its ideas permeated the infamous and ill-fated Treaty of Bjorke of 1905 in which Nicholas and Wilhelm II of Germany called upon France to break its alliance with England and join them in an assault upon international Jewry. Nicholas and Alexandra ordered a sermon quoting the pamphlet in all the 368 churches of Moscow, and they supported its publication in right-wing newspapers. The *Protocols* allowed them to think that the Russian people were not dissatisfied with their rule, that the Jews and the Freemasons stood behind the defeat of Russia by Japan in 1905, that the Jews had inspired the mass strikes, and that they had raised the demand for a parliament *(Duma)* and the forty-hour week. The *Protocols* served as a form of self-justification for a rotten theocratic regime and the reversals it experienced amid the Russian Revolution of 1905, which Trotsky appropriately called the "dress rehearsal" for 1917.

The royal couple was genuinely shocked when they learned that the pamphlet was a forgery. No less than more common Russian antisemites, who insisted on an innate Jewish passion for material gain, they were not only hostile to Judaism as a religion, but to Jewry as an ethnic entity or what they considered a racial or nationalistic cult intent on undermining the Empire. It is true that Princess Elisabeth played an important role in dealing with the censors and keeping the book in print,[50] but her task was assuredly not that difficult: the czar and czarina provided a subsidy for publishing the *Protocols* even after they learned that the tract was a fraud.[51] They undoubtedly considered it unfortunate that interest in the pamphlet should have started to wane. Nilus raged at the refusal of the world to take him or his book seriously: Chayla noted how the tract was ignored by most religious journals and reviews; sensible aristocrats claimed that decent people dismissed the book.

But this is all somewhat ingenuous. The *Protocols* may not have been properly appreciated in the eyes of its lunatic editor; it may not have been read by intellectuals; and it makes sense that intelligent aristocrats should have sought to dissociate themselves from the rabble and the Black Hundreds. The pamphlet itself may well not have sold the way it did later. None of this, however, says anything about the popularity of its ideas. These were surely strengthened by the original support rendered the work by the royal couple and its promulgation by the religious community of Moscow. The appearance of the *Protocols* indeed coincided with the eruption of more than a hundred pogroms between 1903 and 1906, mostly instigated by advocates of its ideas among the Black Hundreds. There were more than 5,000 deaths in more than 53 cities and 600 villages in 1905 alone. The massacres in Kishinev and elsewhere,[52] overshadowed by the far greater tragedy of the 1930s, are often forgotten. The *Protocols* played their role in the events whose cruelty is perhaps best summed up by an eyewitness account of what occurred to a single victim:

> He left his wife, who was pregnant, and three children to go on a business trip. When he got back, the massacre had occurred. His home was in ruins, his family gone. He went to the hospital, then to the cemetery. There he found his wife with her abdomen stuffed with straw, and his three children dead. It simply broke his heart, and he lost his mind. But he was harmless: he was seen wandering about the

hospital as though in search of someone, and daily he grew more thin and suffering.[53]

Antisemitism was no better, and probably much worse, in Russia than it was in Germany, especially in the years following the catastrophic war with Japan. Between 1905 and 1906, Russia witnessed the dissemination of over 14 million copies of roughly 3,000 antisemitic books and pamphlets with the czar himself contributing over 12 million rubles to the enterprise.[54] Accusations by influential governmental officials associated with the Black Hundreds concerning the "blood libel," the belief that Jews murdered Christian youths for the use of their blood in secret rituals, created an international scandal during the notorious Beiliss Affair of 1911.[55] Occasional pogroms continued to take place and democratic life in the country withered. In the decades preceding World War I, however, the nation experienced a sense of torpor perhaps best illustrated in the plays of Anton Chekhov. The *Protocols* went into hibernation. And that is unsurprising: the pamphlet had no purpose to serve during these years of relative quiet. That would change soon enough.

THE *PROTOCOLS* GO TO WAR

The *Protocols* needed a purpose to serve: the First World War provided one. The mystery was real enough. Prior to 1914, after all, foreign policy was carried out through "secret diplomacy." None of the decisions made by the elites, of course, had anything to do with the machinations of Jews and Freemasons: indeed, hardly a single Jew held a position of genuine political authority anywhere on the continent. But this mattered little. The *Protocols* offered a mythical explanation, functional for certain groups and classes, that blamed the war on a secret cabal of Jews and the introduction of modernity on the Jewish spirit.

Any serious analysis, of course, must begin differently. The First World War was the culmination of old great power rivalries and imperialist policies that ultimately reach back to the defeat of

Napoleon.[56] Its architects were of the old school and among those who had trained under the dominant figures of nineteenth-century diplomacy—Andrassy, Bismarck, Cavour, Disraeli, and Gorchakov.[57] All the major actors on the international stage wished to maintain the existing balance of power and, simultaneously, retain the right to intervene in the affairs of smaller states and strengthen their position through imperialism. The First World War was initiated by old men. None of them had either the ability or the will to challenge the tendencies leading to war. Most of those in power mistakenly employed the Franco-Prussian War of 1870-71, which only lasted six months, as their point of reference. None of them were really able to envision what a *world war* would entail. As alliances between the great powers shifted, however, more than eleven million square miles were added to the colonial possessions of the great European powers during the forty years leading up to World War I.[58] This brought nations to the brink of war and then back again. The *Protocols* provides the sense, if not the analysis, of a world teetering on the edge of an abyss.

Even following the assassination of the Archduke Ferdinand at Sarajevo in 1914, however, there was nothing inevitable about the outbreak of war. The problem lay in the paralyzing fatalism that had been strengthened by a seemingly endless string of crises caused primarily by conflicting imperialist ambitions: two confrontations in Morocco no less than the limited wars in Bosnia in 1908 and the Balkan Wars of 1912-13 had previously almost escalated into conflagrations of a more universal sort. These crises produced an ostensibly iron logic through which Europe was led to war: the agent for this development remained hidden, or difficult to comprehend, which ultimately heightened the appeal of simplistic and conspiratorial explanations like those offered by *Protocols*.

The pamphlet reduced both international and domestic decisions to a single invisible source and thereby, in a perverse way, it partially reflected something genuine. International competition between states and domestic class conflict did, in fact, reinforce one another. Images of what Jose Ortega y Gasset would later call a "revolt of the masses" were uppermost in the minds of the upper classes. The decades preceding World War I were marked everywhere in Europe by the extraordinary rise of the socialist labor movement with its commitment to republicanism and social justice. French reactionaries could still recall the Paris Commune, Austria-Hungary and Germany were plagued by the ever more impressive electoral victories of social democracy, and Russia was recovering from the Revolution of 1905. Constitutionalism and economic demands for redistribution were everywhere threatening the power of entrenched aristocratic elites, while new ideological preoccupations with science and materialism were calling into question established customs and religious beliefs. Fear became the double mirror in which opposing nations and opposing classes within them saw one another.[59]

War ever more surely appeared not merely as a tactic capable of contesting the imperialist ambitions of other nations abroad, but also as a way to counteract the new demands of the toiling masses at home. This claim seemed bold when it was first made in the 1920s by the great liberal historian Elie Halévy in *The Era of the Tyrannies.* The czar and the Kaiser saw a Jewish conspiracy working hand in hand with all democratic and socialist forces for the destruction of their homelands.[60] And the purpose of the Jews was clear. Anti-semites asked: Would the Balfour Declaration of 1917, which established a Zionist Jewish state in Palestine under English protection, have been possible without the destruction of Imperial Germany and Imperial Russia?[61]

The Imperialist, a staunchly right-wing journal, claimed in 1918, when the outcome of the war was still uncertain, that the House of Windsor along with British residents of German background were plotting with representatives of an "international conspiracy" of Jews and homosexuals to hand over England to the Germans. The notorious antisemite, Leslie Fry, published a resoundingly paranoiac foreword to the *Protocols* while Henry Ford explained in *The International Jew* that the Jews had plotted the death of Archduke Ferdinand and caused nations to mobilize. He claimed that Jewish newspapers had whipped up a war frenzy, that Jewish financiers had profited from the slaughter, and that Jewish agitators had brought the

United States into the war. The *Protocols* indeed "fit" the historical situation: the Jews were the scourge of Europe.

Antisemitism grew with the disappearance of the initial euphoria attendant on the outbreak of war in 1914. Trench warfare, profiteering, financial speculation, massive military mismanagement, divisions among politicians, a disastrous peace treaty, the influx of Jews from the East—all seemed explicable by reference to traditional stereotypes of Jews fostered by the new paramilitary and agitational organizations of the far right. The enemy at home was the same as the enemy abroad. "The International Jew," to use Henry Ford's phrase, had aroused national passions, pitted one country against another, and profited from the conflict between them—before the war by making munitions; during the war by floating national loans; and after the war by creating a "free for all" in which all nations must bid for the materials controlled by the outsider.[62]

The *Protocols* predicted it all. Or so it seemed. Its vision of war and moral collapse, economic convulsion and political revolution, social decay and cultural confusion must have seemed prophetic to those already inclined to believe in the tract. The chaos attendant on the war was sufficient to justify the authenticity of the pamphlet, and its authenticity, in turn, was sufficient to justify belief in a Jewish cabal. The thinking was tautological. But that didn't matter. The Jew *caused* the war; the Jew *betrayed* the nation. It didn't matter that in Germany 100,000 Jews participated in the war and 78,000 served time at the front; it was irrelevant that 12,000 lost their lives in battle, and that 30,000 received medals for bravery.[63] The *Protocols* revealed a different truth. Catastrophe had occurred, "the Jew" was behind it. That was enough.

FIVE

Spreading the News:
The *Protocols* Triumphant

World War I was begun by the great powers without ideals or clearly defined interests, and it ended with a continent in ruins.[1] Beyond the thirty-eight million dead and maimed, beyond the previously unimaginable devastation, its victims included those upon whom the learned elders of Zion had promised to wreak their vengeance. Four empires were destroyed whose roots reached back more than a thousand years: the Austro-Hungarian, the German, the Ottoman, and the Russian. The war decimated the *ancien régime*. Established traditions were overturned and a corrosive cynicism was generated among much of the population. In an epoch marked by chaos and transition, it was little wonder that the *Protocols* should have gained such popularity.

World War I was an irrational escape from domestic pressures rather than a way of pursuing attainable goals. Unable to meet the demands of reform at home, the legitimization of the old elites ever more surely rested on the ability to bring about spectacular successes abroad. Its members could neither admit the senselessness of the conflict nor expose their culpability. This would have meant tossing themselves upon the "trash can of history" and belittling the "brotherhood of the trenches." It was only logical that the old elites should have sought to highlight the organic unity of the nations, which they claimed to represent, and blame an outsider or traitor for the slaughter they had brought about. They could not deal with the implications of imperialism, militarism, class conflict, and a stubborn reactionary political structure incapable of reform. Virtually all conservatives and militant reactionaries, especially those on the losing side, needed to justify themselves both politically and existentially. Indeed, when the spectacular successes were not forthcoming, it was necessary to provide a reason for the defeats and a source for the mistaken policy: antisemitism provided both.

Nowhere was this more the case than in Imperial Russia. Its economic situation 1914 was still woeful by western standards; its masses of peasants in the countryside and proletarians in the city were impoverished; its army poorly trained and staffed; its resources insufficient for a protracted struggle. But this did not keep the czar and czarina, who quarreled constantly over the Balkans with the doddering Emperor Franz Joseph of Austria-Hungary from being among the prime instigators of World War I. The defeats came quickly. Nevertheless, the pitifully incompetent rulers of Russia were willing to suffer increasing losses in order to maintain their tumbling prestige.

The czar and czarina remained firm in their convictions. They never doubted their royal prerogatives or the divine legitimization of their rule. And so, when the revolution finally struck, they were left in a daze. Its first phase in February of 1917, which resulted in the formation of a provisional government led by Alexander Kerensky, was hard for the aristocracy and other stalwarts of the old regime to swallow; the second phase, the Bolshevik seizure of power in November, left them in a state of utter incomprehension. Indeed, if the Jews didn't exist, the far right would probably have invented a functional equivalent to blame for the catastrophe.

World War I forced modernity down the throats of even the most recalcitrant. Czar Nicholas and Kaiser Wilhelm could only have despised both progressive political alternatives of modernity generated in the wake of World War I and against which the *Protocols* had preached: a republic predicated on the rule of law *(Rechtsstaat)* and a dictatorship of the proletariat committed to eradicating the traditions and privileges of the old regime. Neither form of government had any use for them or their kind, for divine right of kings or the established church, for an agricultural society and traditional mores.

Not only the supporters of these old monarchs, however, but also the more radical partisans of a burgeoning fascist movement found themselves cast adrift. They were left to oppose both the new continental republics, whose liberal capitalist institutions were buttressed by a social democratic mass base, and an authoritarian communist movement intent on realizing a new form of economic equality. A seemingly unstoppable "wind from the East" and an apparently triumphant spirit of democracy in the West left them alienated from the working class and the political system in which they would be forced to operate.

The *Protocols* was, by itself, insufficient for the formation of a new fascist worldview. Its vision of a reinvigorated aristocracy and its dream of political restoration lay shattered amid the rubble of the trenches. Indeed, even before World War I, there were indications among authoritarian radicals that the time of the aristocracy was past and that compromise with the existing order was impossible: French authoritarians living in the hated Third Republic, which lasted from 1871 until 1940, were already seeking less a return to feudalism than a dictatorship led by a military "hero" like General Boulanger. Italian futurists, antidemocratic if not antisemitic, pilloried the aristocracy and the remnants of a noble past. Imperialist segments of the German right were also beginning to view the aristocratic *Junkers* as an anachronism, and Hitler spent the years prior to World War I in Vienna fuming against the decaying Habsburg monarchy.

None of this is meant to deny that much of the political right remained traditionalist or that a certain nostalgia was often apparent when thinking about the imperial regimes of the prewar period. The forces of reaction were not yet led by genuine revolutionaries as Europe emerged from the debris of World War I. Monarchists like General Denikin of the White Russian Army during the civil war and General Erich Ludendorff, who commanded the German Army during World War I, were the points of reference for men and women of the right. But, still, *romantic* nostalgia for the past was beginning to make way for a new *neoromantic* vision concerned with the creation of a racially homogeneous community of the people *(Volksgemeinschaft)*. The traditional sense of piety and place, the primacy of church and feudal status, was irrelevant to the more callous and cynical perspectives of hardened war veterans and alienated youth, *Lumpenproletarians* and embittered bohemians, *déclassé* bourgeois and disillusioned intellectuals.

The most bold and prescient partisans of the right realized that the new people's community demanded new leadership and new beliefs. Its most radical elements surrendered the more aristocratic pretensions and religious convictions of their more establishmentarian brethren in the aftermath of World War I. And, initially, it might seem that advocates of the *Protocols* had backed the wrong horse. Nilus began one of his postwar editions with the claim that "political problems can only be comprehended by rulers who have been directing affairs for centuries." It was the same with Gottfried zur Beek, when he introduced the German edition of the *Protocols* in 1919. Vigorously sponsored by scions of the German nobility like Prince Otto von Salm, Prince Joachim Albrecht of Prussia, and even by the ex-Kaiser Wilhelm II who recommended it to his visitors at Doorn, the pamphlet was dedicated: "To the Princes of Europe."[2]

Tensions steadily grew between the romantic reactionaries and partisans of a monarchical order and the new neoromantic revolutionaries of the right. But, strangely, the popularity of the *Protocols* grew apace as the 1920s turned into the 1930s and as the Weimar Republic, over the corpse of a divided left, gave way before the life-and-death struggle between fascists and an antifascist Popular Front in France and Spain. The economic ideas of the *Protocols* were antiquated at best and completely incoherent at worst. It also offered no positive positions relevant for a new counterrevolutionary organization or movement on the rise. Even ideologically, with respect to antisemitism, the document lacked the primitive biological and pseudoscientific foundations so admired by more modern bigots like Adolf Hitler. Still, it contributed mightily to the formation of a right-wing worldview in the interwar period. The *Protocols* became a bridge between the old and the new right.

The pamphlet gained in notoriety precisely because it was distributed with a new proficiency, and because it became an ideological weapon in a concerted international right-wing assault on the republican state. The *Protocols* indeed served as a type of handbook for action. It imparted a sense of political urgency into the new "scientific" discussions of antisemitism and put the political battle against the Jews on the historical agenda. In the language of Georges Sorel,[3] the pamphlet provided a "myth": a sense of peril, a motivation for action, a heroic self-understanding, and a justification for violence. Its very inadequacies, combined with its critical assault against those who would temporize on the Jewish question, forced the far right to rethink its worldview. It thereby engendered the need to formulate a new magical past as a response to "Jewish" modernity and to invent a new racialist form of integral nationalism as a response to "Jewish" cosmopolitanism. All this made the *Protocols* crucial for those intent upon resisting the apparently triumphant political trends of East and West.[4]

AGAINST EAST AND WEST

The *Protocols* appeared at a time when republican aspirations were in the air and the socialist labor movement was experiencing an international burst of growth. Marxism was the movement's guiding ideology and during its "golden age,"[5] which extended from 1889 until 1914, socialist support for the values of republican democracy was unambiguous. Every prominent socialist prior to the Russian Revolution identified the "dictatorship of the proletariat," if they accepted the concept at all, either with a republic or even more participatory forms of organization such as "soviets" or "workers' councils." The basic idea of marxism, which centered on the belief that the proletariat would grow while all other classes would shrink, was precisely what made the vision of a democratic order so appealing. The problem would indeed always be less the antisemitic character of the socialist labor movement than its marxian optimism regarding an "inevitable" victory of the proletariat and its subsequent underestimation of antisemitic political movements generated by incompatible interests and jumbled ideological claims.[6]

Republicanism and socialism were the two great progressive ideological expressions of the Enlightenment and reactionaries traditionally identified both with Jewish interests. Although it is foolish to link them by referring to a Jewish agenda, interestingly enough, these ideas actually stood in a coherent relation with one another. In fact, since a politically self-confident bourgeoisie was lacking nearly everywhere on the continent for most of the nineteenth century, the principal supporter of republicanism became the western socialist labor movement. This weakness of bourgeois liberalism became apparent in the Weimar Republic, in which social democracy essentially served as the mass base for republican politics. The liberal German Democratic Party (DDP), which emerged in 1919 as the third strongest force in the new republic, sunk in the 1920s as a result of reactionary attacks—it was often criticized as the "Party of the Jews"—and it was transformed from an important actor on the parliamentary scene into an impotent sect. The decline of the Jewish role in German life during the interwar period is reflected in the decline of the liberal party.[7]

Historically, Jews had been engaged in various political movements: many were liberals, others were conservatives, some were Zionists, and a significant number were drawn to Italian fascism before the introduction of racial laws in 1938.[8] They were, however, disproportionately drawn to the left. Well-known socialists of Jewish origin included Eduard Bernstein, Léon Blum, Theodor Dan, Julius Martov, and Rosa Luxemburg. As for the communists, Nikolai Bukharin, Lev Kamenev, Karl Radek, Grigory Zinoviev, and Leon Trotsky counted among the most important leaders of the new movement, while Lenin was considered by most right-wing extremists as a Jew in disguise. Jews were thus prominent in the leadership of the two wings of the labor movement.

But these now confronted one another as deadly enemies. World War I had created an irrevocable breach, or what Blum appropriately termed a basic "moral incompatibility," between them. National support by social democratic parties for the war effort in the West had led radicals to embrace a revolutionary communist movement in the East that demanded unconditional allegiance to its authoritarian "dictatorship of the proletariat."

All this meant little to the antisemites and the forces of reaction. They didn't care about Lenin's condemnation of the western "labor aristocracy" and they simply ignored the contention of socialist intellectuals that communist suppression in February 1917 of the democratic provisional government headed by Alexander Kerensky, which censored all publication of the *Protocols,* would result in a dynamic of repression and terror.[9] Bourgeois republic and proletarian dictatorship meant the same thing to the partisans of the extreme right. The Jews provided the bridge between them. Indeed, only by solidifying this connection could aristocratic conservatives and right-wing extremists make sense of the dominating event of their era.

The Russian Revolution was followed in 1918 by the start of a brutal civil war in which the republican option vanished: it created the need for a simple choice between Reds and Whites. Most Jews sought only peace and an escape from a conflict whose barbarity was extreme even by the standards of the day. When forced to choose the lesser evil, however, most supported the Bolsheviks against the staunchly antisemitic Whites. This, in turn, only confirmed the belief perpetrated by new editions of the *Protocols* that the Jews were behind both the bourgeois provisional government, supported by liberals and socialists, and the proletarian dictatorship. The two phases of the revolution had seemingly become one and, viewing the Jews as solidifying the connection between them, the *Protocols* provided the extreme right with a way of explaining in its own terms what Trotsky called "the permanent revolution."

The *Protocols* had warned against the socialists and now its predictions were being validated by the communists with their monopoly over the media, transformation of education, and assault upon the church. The Russian Revolution was understood by the far right as a crucial phase in the expansion of Jewish power or, better, as the culmination of a plan for world conquest initiated by Jews at the very beginning of western civilization. Dietrich Eckart, who would edit the notoriously antisemitic *Völkischer Beobachter* during the early years of the Nazi movement, indeed gave expression to this sentiment in his posthumously published brochure *Bolshevism from Moses to Lenin: A Dialogue between Adolf Hitler and Me.*[10] This idea might even have played a role in bringing about intervention in the civil war from the western powers on behalf of the Whites. Thus, from England in 1921, Lucien Wolf could write:

> It is incredible, but it is nevertheless a fact, that these crazy forgeries played a part behind the scenes in the international combinations for assisting the anti-Bolshevist reaction in Russia, which have filled so much of the public mind during the last two years, and which have cost this country close on 100,000,000 pounds. There was a moment when the Great Powers were disposed to leave the Russians to fight out their quarrels among themselves. Various objections to this policy were urged by the friends of Admiral Koltchak and General Denikin, and among them was the argument that there was, in fact, no civil war in Russia, that Bolshevism was not Russian, but exclusively alien, the work of international Jews who were themselves the instruments of a worldwide deep-laid conspiracy against Christendom and the political order of Europe.[11]

Such beliefs turned the ensuing civil war in the Soviet Union into something more than a struggle of epic proportions between Whites and Reds: it became understood instead by many as a battle between the forces of Christianity and the Jewish Antichrist. The assassination of the czar along with his family by the Bolsheviks in 1918 seemed to confirm this view. The czarina had apparently taken a copy of *The Great in the Small* by Nilus to her last home at Yekaterinburg and, just before her death, she apparently drew a swastika on the wall of the room occupied by the royal couple. It was meant to symbolize the death struggle between Aryans and Jews.[12] Both the book and the sign were discovered at the murder scene. The culprit was clear—the "great" had indeed become evident in the "small."

This interpretation of events in the Soviet Union was not simply confined to fanatics of the old order or partisans of the right in Russia or Germany. The *Times* of London, which would later prove so influential in exposing the forgery of the *Protocols,* initially stated in a long editorial that the pamphlet was genuine. Even more telling is that Winston Churchill could write in the *Illustrated Sunday Herald* of February 8, 1920 that

> this worldwide conspiracy for the overthrow of civilization and for the reconstruction of society on the basis of arrested development, of envious malevolence, and impossible equality has been steadily growing . . . there is no need to exaggerate the part played in the creation of Bolshevism and in the actual bringing about of the Russian Revolution by these international and for the most part atheistical Jews. It is certainly a very great one; it probably outweighs all others.

It would certainly have been easy for the Bolsheviks to play the antisemitic card: thirteen previously warring nations had, after all, sent troops and resources to support the counterrevolution. Nothing would have been simpler than to blame "cosmopolitan Jewry" or "Jewish capital" or "Jewish interests" for the unified assault on the Bolshevik Revolution. To their credit, however, the Reds generally refrained from employing the tactic and even initiated campaigns against antisemitism. Only later under Stalin,[13] and also under Brezhnev, would antisemitism become a major theme: what the Nazis initially termed the conspiracy of Judeo-Communism financed by a Jewish bourgeoisie would then turn into the conspiracy of Judeo-Anticommunism also financed by a Jewish bourgeoisie.

While the civil war raged, antisemitism was an intrinsic element of the White worldview. Three military commanders— Denikin, Kolchak, and Wrangel—were left vying for power following the death of the czar. Each sought popular support and attacks upon the Jews seemed a simple way of securing it. A new edition of the *Protocols* appeared in 1918 and General Denikin's army distributed it among volunteers and the Cossack troops at Kouban. Another edition was printed at Omsk for Admiral Kolchak. The pogroms in the Ukraine and in the Crimea under Wrangel, which are said to have been directly influenced by the appearance of the pamphlet,[14] were terrible in their consequences. Jewish victims during the civil war numbered around 330,000.[15] Rape, pillage, and murder were commonplace and the atrocities were almost incomprehensible in their cruelty. A few accounts from a pogrom near Kiev bear repeating to recall the martyrdom of the victims and the ferocity of those who tortured them.

> I was told of one case of a man being thrown into the fire alive. A man called Kiksman had his tongue cut out and died after being shot with a dumdum bullet. Everyone talks of how dumdum bullets were used, including the medical personnel from the hospital. A man called Markman had both ears cut off, another member of the same family got twelve slashes with a sabre, another got eight. The corpse of a small girl, M. Polskaya, showed that she had suffered burning while alive. One of the lists of the buried (available from the police clerk) contains the names of two six-month-old babies, Avrum Slobodsky and Ruvin Konik. A man was killed by being cut in two. In front of the synagogue about twenty Jews were stripped naked and then shot. . . . Many were hanged until they were dead—for instance Moshko Remenik (on a tree in his garden) and a father and his schoolboy son, Meyer and Boris Zabarsky. These two were experimentally half-hanged first, and the boy was forced to tighten the noose around his father's neck.[16]

Stories of this kind made the rounds in England and on the continent. But they did little to hinder the success of the *Protocols*. Quite the contrary. Its appeal by 1927 was indeed such that Agatha Christie, in one of the mysteries featuring her famous fictional detective Hercule Poirot, could satirically make reference to an international conspiracy and a supposedly horrifying work entitled "The Hidden Hand in China."[17] The economic turmoil produced by the close of the war had created a climate of conspiracy and the civil war in Russia echoed abroad. The *Protocols* gained in popularity everywhere in Europe precisely because roughly the same forces of reaction were engaged in roughly the same crusade to justify themselves in their fight against the republic and the soviet, the bourgeoisie and the proletariat, socialism and capitalism, liberalism and Bolshevism.

Displaced elites and disillusioned masses, especially those devastated by defeat in Austria, Germany, and Hungary, experienced the same fears as their right-wing brethren in Russia. Jewish social democrats were attempting to introduce republican government into what had previously been monarchical regimes even while, in the spirit of 1917, Jewish radicals like Rosa Luxemburg, Béla Kun, and Kurt Eisner were intent upon instituting "soviets" through the Spartacus Revolt in Berlin, the Hungarian rising in Budapest, and the Munich revolt.[18] By 1921, however, Lenin had officially shifted the party line with his pamphlet, *Left-wing Communism: An Infantile Disorder.* The specter of communist revolution receded. The right could now focus its attention upon the democratic states born from what increasingly appeared as a useless conflict. Many of these states stood upon shaky foundations from the time of their inception: this was indeed dramatically the case with the Weimar Republic.[19]

Against the prospect of more radical action from the far left, which threatened the introduction of soviets, Germany's social democratic leadership had secured a compromise in which the prewar imperial elites would formally accept the new regime in exchange for a commitment to maintain existing property relations, the prewar legal and state bureaucracy, and the military leadership. The Weimar Republic was thus built upon a reactionary antirepublican infrastructure. It lacked loyalty among the elites even more than among the populace at large. Contemptuous of democratic politics, faced with a decimated aristocracy, and without any specific agent for social change, the right initially looked back to its political tradition and organized itself in the form of conspiratorial *Ligues* or *Freikorps,* or radically authoritarian political parties buttressed by a host of paramilitary organizations, secret societies, and agitational clubs.[20] Their partisans would indeed prove far more effective at implementing the conspiratorial lessons contained in the *Protocols* than the supposedly all-powerful Elders of Zion they were so intent on combating.

Antisemitism fit their concerns perfectly. All the Christian nations had suffered, winners and losers alike, but the Jews supposedly never had it so good: they were the winners. Everywhere it was believed that the Rothschilds, the Guggenheims, and their agents had plunged Europe into war in order to line their own pockets. In the victorious countries, they had bargained away the "fruits of victory," while in Germany it was common knowledge that, just as the troops were poised for victory, the Jews were preparing the nation for a "stab in the back." Many Germans believed that the Jews had shirked their duty on the front lines, that they had undermined the war effort in order to introduce the despicable Weimar Republic, and that their social democratic and liberal agents, the "November criminals," had almost gleefully signed the hated Treaty of Versailles: only outsiders, such as the Jews, would have called upon Germany to admit its guilt for starting the war and burdened the country with heavy reparations.

A political identity crisis was sparked with the introduction of the Weimar Republic. Germany had been late in becoming a nation and it lacked a forceful democratic tradition.[21] The new republic brought with it universal suffrage, an indeterminate notion of citizenship, and a new emphasis on Enlightenment values. Parties now represented particular concerns rather than those of the nation, interest groups flourished, and it seemed that there was no representative of the common good, no existential feeling of national unity. As George Mosse noted:

> Middle-class complacency and struggle for wealth, symbolized by the corruption of parliamentary government, seemed to exemplify the victory of materialism over the nation. The materialism of the establishment confronted the materialism of the socialists. The struggle for ever greater wealth threatened to divide the nation. In order to counter the menace from above and below, the ideal of the national community was transformed into a third force, supposedly transcending both capitalist and socialist materialism.[22]

It increasingly became an article of faith among the forces of reaction that the republic was an alien system imposed by an alien entity upon the "people's community." The hyperinflation accompanying the republic's introduction, which the *Protocols* considered a unique weapon of the Jews, didn't help matters. Right-wing extremists blamed the phenomenon on an international Jewish cabal intent upon further weakening an already defeated Germany. Their attack on Jews logically translated into an attack upon "the Jew republic." Thus, what began as the reactionary defense against communism in the East soon enough turned into an unrelenting assault upon the democratic legacy of the West.

THE *PROTOCOLS* ON THE MARCH

Fascism was a revolt against reason in the name of the senses. An alternative to modern ideologies and a revolt against the dominant classes in the modern production process, the bourgeoisie and the proletariat, it offered salvation from the economic chaos, the class conflict, and the decline of authority during the turbulent 1920s. Its partisans everywhere called for an authoritarian state, identified themselves with the national will, cast opprobrium upon the outsider, and always found a scapegoat. They extolled the arbitrary power exercised by a new leader with mythical powers, a *Duce* or a *Führer,* and their ideology everywhere lauded action for its own sake, war for the sake of war, and death for the sake of death.[23] Indeed, the partisans of fascism were ultimately less concerned with securing established tradition, or even "law and order," than initiating a "national revolution."

Not every traditional antisemite was a fascist and not every fascist was an antisemite, but the two positions reinforced one another. Fascist ideology seemed to many a way of reinvigorating the more traditional politics of antisemitism by infusing it with a new missionary, almost religious, fervor. Contempt for modernity and the Enlightenment heritage created what Max Weber would have termed an "elective affinity" between more traditional conservatives and fascists. The enemies of fascism were, moreover, generally the same as those of more established elites. Traditionalists were generally driven to panic by the Reds and their "Jewish" leaders. They were as committed to a homogeneous people's community, and most were as sharply critical of the cultural "decadence" and liberal spirit associated with the republicanism as the partisans of the more extreme right.

This was not only the case in Germany where Catholic and Protestant churches heartily recommended the *Protocols* to their parishioners, which often led to pogroms in the countryside, and warned against the "alien entity" inside the German *Volk*.[24] Hungary under the rule of Admiral Horthy from 1919-44 was explicitly antiliberal and antisocialist in orientation and its "Christian nationalism," which was endorsed by conservatives and fascists alike, really reflected little more than an official slogan for antisemitism. Italy witnessed a *concordat* between Mussolini and the pope, while in Spain the Catholic Church and the fascist *Falange*, which would sponsor its own version of the *Protocols*, were allies from the beginning of what would become an assault on the Republic in 1936. The *Action Française* gained increasing support in France from more established conservatives during the 1920s and 1930s even while a staunch antisemitic movement known as the *Rassemblement Anti-Juif* unsuccessfully sought to build a united front among antisemites. Supporters of this latter organization, in particular, dedicated themselves to fighting the "international Jewish conspiracy" and viewed the *Protocols* as "'certain' confirmation of the crimes and powers they had already ascribed to the Jews."[25]

Antisemitic fears in postwar Europe were only exacerbated when the battle in the fledgling Soviet Union was finally decided and White émigrés flooded the continent. They settled in the great cities like Paris and Berlin, made contacts with anticommunist and antiliberal groups, and spurred a craze for Dostoyevsky and Russian mysticism among young right-wing extremists. These included Hermann Rauschning, who understood Nazism as the "revolution of nihilism," and Arthur Moeller van den Bruck whose name would become associated with the idea of a "Third Reich." Not only the left, but also the right, was feeling the "wind from the East" in the aftermath of the war. It is indeed useful to consider that the cynical and conspiratorial approach to politics, which the Nazis found in the *Protocols*, could well have been reinforced by the words of the grand inquisitor in Dostoyevsky's *The Brothers Karamazov* or the nihilists in another of his great works, *The Possessed.*[26]

Especially given the rancor generated by recent attempts to depict the holocaust as the function of a uniquely German tradition of antisemitism,[27] it is important to highlight that the single most politically significant antisemitic work of the interwar period, the *Protocols,* was not a German invention employed by right-wing Germans to detonate the Enlightenment spirit. It was instead an export brought into Germany by émigrés from Imperial Russia, among them, Alfred Rosenberg. A Baltic German of ultraright views, who would later become the chief ideologist of the Nazis and Reichsminister for the Eastern Provinces,[28] he carried the pamphlet in his suitcase when he left Estonia for Munich in 1918. Apparently, one year earlier, a stranger had placed the brochure on his desk at the university and then vanished.[29] Soon after his arrival, Rosenberg came into contact with Dietrich Eckart and Rudolf Hess, the future "deputy of the *Führer*," and his new friends immediately embraced the document.

Eckert and Hess were members of the Thule Society, which was founded in 1918 and harked back to the Germanic-Thule Sect of 1912. It mingled a belief in the occult with an infatuation for Aryan and Germanic myths. A secret organization, at the center of right-wing extremism in Munich, it published numerous antisemitic leaflets and brochures in great numbers and at minimal cost.[30] The Thule Society brought out the *Protocols* in 1919, with a scholarly preface by Ludwig Müller under the pseudonym Gottfried zur Beek which made no mention of Nilus, under the auspices of the League Against Jewish Arrogance.[31] It was a tremendous success. The pamphlet immediately sold more than 120,000 copies and it quickly became known as "the Bible of antisemites" in Germany.

Hitler may ultimately have grown to despise Rosenberg, who interestingly enough became a driving force in the attempt to rid German culture and art of its Jewish influences, and he probably never read his party philosopher's sprawling *Myth of the Twentieth Century,* which was obviously inspired by the *Protocols.* But the future *Führer* was surely influenced by Rosenberg after the two met in

Munich in 1920. Obsessed by the omnipresence of dark powers working behind the scenes, clearly paranoiac, Rosenberg would publish his own edition of the *Protocols* in 1940. A shortened version of the pamphlet, however, appeared in the *Völkischer Beobachter* on February 25, 1920: it was the day after the meeting in which Hitler first articulated his program. Other meetings would soon be given over to the analysis offered by the *Protocols,* and its themes later became staples in the speeches of Nazi leaders against the Weimar Republic. A Jewish reporter noted,

> In Berlin I attended several meetings which were entirely devoted to the Protocols. The speaker was usually a professor, a teacher, an editor, a lawyer or someone of that kind. The audience consisted of members of the educated class, civil servants, tradesmen, former officers, ladies, above all students, students of all faculties and years of seniority . . . Passions were whipped up to the boiling point.[32]

The *Protocols* crystallized the qualitatively different opponents of the right into a single enemy responsible for all the ills of modernity, and imputed to that enemy a plan for world domination. It also handed the right an explanation for an inexplicable global conflict, marked by incompetent military leadership and an extraordinary waste of lives and material, as well as for the outbreak of the Russian Revolution and, later, the Great Depression of 1929. Without any concern for facts or verification, it offered seemingly practical reasons for an international assault upon the Jews. Heinrich Himmler, recuperating from an illness in 1919, was apparently influenced by an antisemitic work based on the *Protocols* in which Jews, Freemasons, and Democrats were reviled as the agents of world revolution, and he noted in his diary that this was "a book that explains everything and tells us whom we must fight against next time."[33]

It has been noted often how the pamphlet informed the outlook of the Nazis and the actions of those who murdered Walter Rathenau—the famous writer, industrialist, and foreign minister of Germany[34]—on June 24, 1922.[35] Among the defendants were members of the Thule Society who expressly referenced the *Protocols* and who believed that Rathenau was among the leading "elders of Zion." He had become known for his quip that "300 men control the destiny of Europe," and his wealth made him suspect; he was castigated for selling Germany out to its former enemies by calling for adherence to the reparations policy dictated by the Treaty of Versailles; his support for the Treaty of Rapallo, which sought to secure relations with Russia, led to accusations that he was an agent for the Bolsheviks. Idiotic rumors also circulated that he had given his sister over in marriage to the famous revolutionary Karl Radek. Above all, however, Rathenau incarnated the image of the Jew portrayed in the *Protocols:* a fabulously rich cosmopolitan intellectual, working behind the scenes, at the summit of political power. The famous ditty made the rounds: "Knallt ab den Walter Rathenau, die gottverdammte Judensau!" (Knock off Walter Rathenau, the goddamned Jewish sow!)

The assassination of Rathenau was a dramatic moment in the history of the Weimar Republic. But to isolate the incident or to highlight the importance of the *Protocols* in motivating the murder of this particular Jew is to miss the point. His assassination and the functional role of the *Protocols* must be understood in the context of an ongoing war against the partisans of republicanism and the labor movement. The same public calls to murder were directed against Luxemburg and Liebknecht, who were murdered in 1919, along with other prominent Jewish social democrats like Hugo Haase and Kurt Eisner, ultraleft Jewish radicals like Gustav Landauer and Eugen Leviné, and the Catholic liberal Matthias Erzberger. A spirit of intolerance was palpable and violence was endemic to the new republic; street fights between Communists and Nazis were daily occurrences for much of its history. But crimes by the extreme right far outnumbered those committed on the left and the criminals could generally anticipate far more lenient treatment. It was indeed possible to speak about a vast right-wing conspiracy against the Weimar Republic and the *Protocols* provided an organizational handbook for the rebels.

Albert Camus suggested in his play *Caligula* (1938) that the totalitarian mind is predicated on the idea that everything is possible.

In this vein, the *Protocols* depicts a world conspiracy though, in contrast to its claims, the project was actually undertaken by fascists rather than Jews. The pamphlet was surely one source from which the Nazis gained a sense that world domination is possible and that the endeavor rests upon the willingness to deal ruthlessly with opponents and the ability to secure the unconditional loyalty of followers. Especially in France, well-known if politically perverse literary figures like Pierre Drieu la Rochelle, Robert Brasillach, and Louis-Ferdinand Céline used the *Protocols* in order to justify their belief in the organic, the national, the mythical, the irrational, or their opportunistic collaboration with the Nazis.[36] It was the same elsewhere: Ezra Pound, Knut Hamsun, and Ernst Jünger were inspired by it as well to justify similar ideas in similar fashion.

More important, however, was the way that the *Protocols* inspired the political strategy of an entire movement. The mass disorganization of society supposedly advocated by the Jews was put into practice by those who became their persecutors. The fascist demand for order was always accompanied by a policy intent upon spreading disorder. Intimidation of opponents became a favored tactic along with the assassination of public figures. Perversion of the public sphere, concerted use of propaganda, and use of the big lie all became elemental tactics. No charge was too outlandish, no tactic too outrageous, no goal too ambitious. The Nazis condemned the Jews for starting mass uprisings and undermining the state even as they ceaselessly plotted the seizure of power. They raised paranoid suspicions about the secret organizations of the Jews even as they created their own private army funded by elites from behind the scenes. No less than the "elders of Zion," the Nazis employed the civil liberties of democracy in order to bring about its downfall. Indeed, they too would infuse antisemitism with a religious fervor in order to ideologically buttress their quest for power.

The *Protocols* offered its readers a Manichean vision: it was now a matter of Aryan against Jew, us against them, or in the words of Charles Peguy, "Occidental revolt" against "Oriental fatalism." Other right-wing leaders had used antisemitism in their march to power, and fascism had already brought other republics to their knees. But Hitler was the first to focus his movement against a single enemy who was supposedly controlling all his other enemies: his *absolute state* would rest upon the struggle against an *absolute enemy*. And this was totally in keeping with the thrust of the *Protocols*. He was surely aware of its emphasis upon developing new "leaders." The irony is unmistakable: the "elders of Zion" were transmuted into the inner circle of the Nazi party while the chief rabbi of the Jews turned into the *Führer* of the Germans. What Theodor Adorno called the "truth content" of the work became manifest in the lies it told. The *Protocols* make it possible to understand the coherence behind a seemingly incoherent strategy committed to insane ends.

THE *PROTOCOLS* ON TRIAL

Many still wonder how antisemitism, which had essentially been a relatively marginal political phenomenon during the prewar years, could have gained such dominance in the interwar era. It had previously been "at best a rough and unwieldy political device, even in tsarist Russia."[37] But things changed following the Russian Revolution and the economic crisis attendant upon the conclusion of World War I. The appeal of antisemitism was strengthened by the Great Depression of 1929 and the sensational financial scandals of the 1930s, like the Stavisky Affair in France. Other factors, however, were also involved. The interwar years witnessed a concerted effort to highlight antisemitism in the right-wing struggle against the republican status quo. This does not mean that every assault upon democracy undertaken in the 1920s and 1930s was antisemitic, but it does mean that every antisemitic organization was committed to the destruction of democracy. Indeed, for the first time, antisemitism became endowed with a revolutionary *political* purpose even as it was *culturally* espoused with new organizational sophistication by a new international fascist movement.

  Intellectuals and editors worked closely together and coordinated their efforts to assure the success of the *Protocols:* everywhere, the pamphlet was produced and distributed in a professional manner. The pamphlet appeared condensed or excerpted in single page leaflets by the millions, and many leading newspapers, like the *Kreuzzeitung* and the *Deutsche Zeitung,* printed it and debated its merits.[38] New versions of the pamphlet were published in Britain, Denmark, Finland, France, Greece, Hungary, Italy, Poland, Romania, Spain, and South Africa. Russian exiles in Siberia brought the *Protocols* to Japan where it was published in 1924,[39] the Patriarch of Jerusalem called upon his followers to purchase the Arabic translation in 1925, and its themes were discussed on the American radio by populist demagogues like Father Charles Coughlin during the 1930s. General Francisco Franco used the *Protocols* to justify a rebellion against the existing republic that would save the "true Spain" from anarchists, atheists, communists, and a "Judeo-Masonic conspiracy." Some versions and interpretations of the pamphlet were more disgusting than others.[40] All of them, however, made the same point regarding Jewish plans for world conquest and assaulted the Enlightenment legacy.

Battle lines had been drawn in the international arena between fascists and antifascists long before 1933: it was not as if the victory of fascism was somehow preordained or as if there were no opponents of principle willing to take the fight into the streets and into the realm of public opinion. The struggle was carried on in the underground work of Italian antifascists following the victory of Mussolini in 1922 as surely as in literary attempts to undermine Nazi appropriations of symbolic figures of the past, like Goethe or Nietzsche, or in the polling booths of Paris during the election of a Popular Front government and on the front lines in the Spanish Civil War. Just as there was a certain international coordination among fascists, whatever the shifting and often devious role played by the communists, a certain solidarity also existed among antifascists.

Jews played an important role in this enterprise. It should subsequently come as no surprise that prominent members of the Swiss Jewish community launched an attack against the *Protocols*. It began in 1933 when a suit was brought for libel and distributing "smut literature" *(Schundliteratur)* against Georg Bernhard Haller, editor-in-chief of the Nazi-oriented paper *Confederates of the Oath (Eidgenossen),*[41] and its publisher Theodor Fischer. They were sued for the articles in their paper affirming the truth of the *Protocols*. Also named were Theodor Fritsch and Gottfried zur Beek, who died before the trial began. Other individuals accused included Silvio Schnell who served as the Swiss editor of the *Protocols* and, finally the prominent architect and member of the National Front, Walter Aebersold. All of them immediately disclaimed any personal responsibility and, in a way, they were irrelevant to the proceedings.[42] The real enemies were the Swiss National Front, the Union of Swiss National Socialists, and most importantly their sponsor, German Nazism.

The Bern trial began in the last week in October of 1934. It started roughly around the time that a similar proceeding against the South African fascists, the Grey Shirts, was being successfully concluded in favor of the Jewish plaintiffs. Officially, the Nazi state refused to intervene. But that did not prevent it from employing the fiercely antisemitic publicist Ulrich Fleischhauer to organize support for the defendants. Even while the domestic strategy was initially left in the hands of Ubald von Roll, the official leader of the Bern section of the Swiss National Front, and his deputy Boris Todtli, Fleischhauer increasingly took charge of the proceedings and his "expert" report to the court on the "inner truth" of the *Protocols* became an antisemitic classic.

The defendants were, obviously, in a difficult position: they had to authenticate what they themselves knew was a fraudulent document. They chose not to call witnesses of their own and instead they concentrated on demeaning the plaintiffs and their supporters. They could not prove any relationship between the Jews and the Freemasons, nor could they produce any evidence capable of substantiating the authenticity of the *Protocols* or discrediting the evidence brought by the other side. They became enmeshed in different versions of how the *Protocols* came into existence. Maintaining that Maurice Joly was actually born a Jew named Moishe Joel, they had little to say when his birth certificate was entered into evidence. Questioned on the claim by Goedsche that the twelve tribes of Israel had met, they were dumfounded when it was noted that only the tribes of Jehuda and Benjamin had survived the destruction of the Second Temple.

When confronted with their claim that the stenographed protocols of the First Zionist Congress were the origins of the *Protocols,* they could not explain why they had not been drafted in German which was the official language of the congress. In fact, when the new 1934 edition of the *Protocols* was published in Leipzig by the Hammer Verlag, it abandoned the original Nazi theory that the pamphlet constituted the records of the first Zionist Congress and that, instead, it was the record of a "secret meeting" of the B'nai B'rith. And so it went. Basically, the defense came down to a tautology: the *Protocols* are authentic because the Jews are evil, and the Jews are evil because the pamphlet says so.[43]

The defense had no other choice than to turn the trial for libel into a political trial. And this meant employing the traditional fascist approach: they disrupted the proceedings, intimidated witnesses, and threatened to countersue them for libel. They asked questions regarding why the Jews had no homeland and they falsified claims about Jewish rituals. They sought to challenge witnesses by pointing to their political affiliations and they impugned experts with wild accusations. They claimed that Jews could not speak the truth and that the trial was controlled by the Jewish conspiracy. It was impossible, they argued, for the defenders of the Aryan race to get justice when faced with such a powerful and organized Jewish opposition. Ultimately, in fact, they sought to argue that the trial was not really about the veracity or falsity of the *Protocols* at all, but rather the "inner truth" it represented regarding a Jewish world conspiracy supported by the Freemasons: it was less about some document than about the political implications deriving from the age-old confrontation between Jews and Aryans.

The situation was different for the Jewish plaintiffs: they were short on funds and lacked manpower. But the legal team, composed of a few historians and leaders of the Swiss Jewish community and led by Georges Brunschvig, proved indefatigable in its commitment. The plaintiffs relied on experts like Arthur Baumgarten and Carl Loosli, the popular Swiss author of *The Bad Jews!* and scholar of the *Protocols,* as well as important Russian historians and former political figures like Boris Nicolayevsky and Paul Miliukov. They employed the testimony of Armand du Chayla. But they also called any number of witnesses who had personal knowledge of the forgery and others like Chaim Weizmann, president of the World Zionist Organization, and Dr. Markus Ehrenpreis, chief rabbi of Stockholm, who could speak to the lack of foundation for any notion of a world conspiracy in either the Jewish religion or Zionism. The plaintiffs made clear that the *Protocols* had been fabricated, that it was copied in numerous handwritings into a notebook with a blue ink spot, that agents of the Russian secret police had ultimately bragged about their undertaking, and that the pamphlet had been plagiarized from the *Dialogue* of Joly and the chapter from *Biarritz* by Goedsche. In short, rationally and without subterfuge, they sought to prove beyond any reasonable doubt that the *Protocols* was a fabrication by antisemites from which the Jewish community had suffered immeasurable harm.

On 14 May 1935 the verdict was delivered: The judge, Walter Meyer, a practicing Christian who had previously never heard of the *Protocols,* found in favor of the plaintiffs. He stated unambiguously that the pamphlet was a forgery and a work of plagiarism; he considered it libelous and a perfect example of "smut literature" that deserved to be banned as incendiary. The Nazis appealed and, unfortunately, a higher court found the definition of "smut literature" identical with sexual pornography under Swiss law. Though the *Protocols* may well be obscene, or so the Court of Appeals argued, it is not obscene in a pornographic sense. Thus, in November 1937, the Court of Appeals overturned the earlier judgment for formal reasons while at the same time confirming the previous finding that the *Protocols* were false and even smut literature in a general sense.

Perhaps it is true that the decision of Judge Meyer is still cited while the appeal has been forgotten.[44] Other trials concerning the authenticity of the *Protocols* took place as recently as 1991 in Johannesburg and 1993 in both Prague and Moscow. But there is a basic way in which the salience of the Swiss legal battle has been overstated. Contempt for the Nazis and sympathy for their victims makes it tempting to dramatize the events. Ignored usually is the political context: the vacillation of the Swiss. Their ongoing attempts to placate their fascist neighbors and their desire to maintain business dealings with the Nazis had resulted in restrictive immigration policies for Jews even as it legitimated antisemitism in their democracy. The two decisions in the trial, indeed, mirror the two souls beating in the heart of Switzerland during the 1930s. Even more generally, however, there is a sense in which Hitler and his friends were correct in their assessment of this trial: it was never simply a fight for the truth. It was, from the first, a political struggle and the arguments concerning the *Protocols*—both pro and con—offered little that was new.

Ernst Bloch liked to explain the appeal of Nazism by citing the words of a Nazi lieutenant: "One does not die for a program that one understands, one dies for a program that one loves."[45] It is the same when dealing with the *Protocols*. The point is not whether they *are* true, but rather whether the antisemite *believes* them to be true. It is easy to forget that the primacy accorded reason, evidence, discourse, and the like were contested by a fascist ideology intent on marshaling the forces of the irrational. Hence the danger of exaggerating the ultimate importance of the trial and overdramatizing the events: the primary appeal of the pamphlet has less to do with proof than prejudice. Hannah Arendt was surely correct when she wrote that:

> . . . if a patent forgery like the "Protocols of the Elders of Zion" is believed by so many people that it can become the text of a whole political movement, the task of the historian is no longer to discover a forgery. Certainly it is not to invent explanations which dismiss the chief political and historical fact of the matter: that the forgery is being believed. This fact is more important than the (historically speaking, secondary) circumstance that it is a forgery.[46]

Whether the *Protocols* was proved a forgery or not ultimately made little difference to future antisemites who, while distributing the pamphlet, often openly admitted its questionable origins. The situation was probably not very different even at the time of the trial: it is difficult to maintain that either the verdict or the appeal actually changed the opinion of anyone. What was truly at stake had already become clear by the end of 1937. Those who had chosen to vacillate, whether from fear or opportunism, would continue to vacillate. The minds of both fascists and antifascists had been made up long before.

TWILIGHT OF THE GODS

The *Protocols* had been thrust into the limelight immediately following the Nazi seizure of power in 1933. It was a time when euphoria ran rampant among supporters of the movement. An assault was immediately undertaken against the cultural vestiges of the Weimar Republic. Hitler feared the spiritual decay of the German *Volk* as much as its material destruction and, from the start, he was committed to eliminating the Jewish influence on public life. The *Protocols* was required reading for the Hitler Youth, trotted out to justify this or that ideological pronouncement, and treated as a classic. The pamphlet served to illustrate "how it could be done,"[47] or how the seizure of power might be accomplished. The fictional conspiracy of the Jews was employed as a model by the Nazis. It served as a warning of what would happen unless the Nazi terror was maintained; it also served as way to justify the war and, later, explain the defeat. Indeed, the *Protocols* retained its ability to incite the masses during the reign of Hitler.[48]

The persecution of German Jews during the 1930s culminated in the infamous *Kristallnacht,* or night of the broken glass. While the excuse for the pogrom was the assassination of the Nazi diplomat Ernst vom Rath in November of 1938[49] by the Polish Jewish student Herschl Grynszpan, the mobilizing slogan employed by the Nazis was still reminiscent of the *Protocols:* "Death to the Jews and the Freemasons." But that wasn't all. In November of 1939, Hitler called for the distribution of the *Protocols* abroad in order to show that the real instigators of the war were the Jews and the Freemasons. It served to justify his preemptive strike against an invisible Jewish conspiracy no less than its democratic and, later, Bolshevik agents. Various versions of the *Protocols* published in the years following World War I, just as the 1917 edition published by Nilus in *It Is Near at Our Doors!,* had indeed warned against the designs of nations like England and the United States directly under the control of Jewish finance.

The *Protocols* identified the Jews as those "pulling the strings" of Germany's disparate enemies from behind the scenes. The enemy within was the same as the enemy without. There was no "place" for the Jews anywhere, using the formulation of Hannah Arendt, and their elimination became the only possible "solution" to the "Jewish question." In this indeterminate sense, the pamphlet can be seen as what has been called a "warrant for genocide." But this should not be taken too far. The *Protocols* fanned the flames of paranoia and it transformed fear into hate. The pamphlet may even have begged the question concerning the introduction of antisemitic policies, many of which had been advocated by traditional antisemites during the early years of the Nazi regime. It was part of a cumulative historical avalanche of antisemitic ideas under which too many corpses were buried. But its vision pales in comparison with the apocalypse envisioned by Hitler and it doesn't even vaguely foreshadow the genocidal practices undertaken by his totalitarian state. The pamphlet never envisioned antisemitism carried through to its logical conclusions by a modern bureaucratic state without aristocratic pretensions: it never projected the merger of technology and myth so important to the Nazis or a more universal theory of racism inclusive of groups other than the Jews; it certainly never envisaged the *genocidal dynamic* so unique to Nazism.[50] The *Protocols* stands in much the same relation to *Mein Kampf* as traditional antisemitism stands to the "final solution" and, perhaps just as disturbingly, the conservatism of the 1920s stands to fascism.

Some trends lead from the past to the present and into the future. Scholars can cull the quotations, point to similarities, and highlight the antisemitic ravings of works like the *Protocols*. It is possible to chart a course leading from the Imperial Court in St. Petersburg to Auschwitz. The warning signs were indisputably there. The *Protocols* basically meets the criteria of what has been called "redemptive antisemitism" insofar as it sees civilization as being corrupted by the Jews and redemption as the liberation from their influence.[51] But the antisemites of a bygone age, like those who had authored the pamphlet, had little regard for the genocidal consequences of their blathering. There were a few in the nineteenth century like Paul Bötticher who considered extermination a solution for the "Jewish problem" though, again, there was little sense about what this might actually imply. The bolder among them spoke about "de-jewification" *(Entjudung)* and Richard Wagner undoubtedly inspired Hitler's imaginings with his intoxicating music and pathological hatred of Jews.[52] A few even ranted about mass murder. Viewing most of the antisemitic cranks from the past or the cynical and semiliterate group of intriguers who forged the *Protocols* as somehow genuinely envisioning the holocaust, however, gives them far too much credit.

None of this lessens their moral culpability. Their horrific ideas, their outlandish claims, their bloody pogroms created the cultural climate in which genocide could blossom. Yet the holocaust is more than the deranged expression of a premodern worldview mired in religious hatred and social prejudice; it is more than the ravings of a pamphlet with nothing to propose for remedying the situation in which the Aryan race supposedly found itself. Everything we have learned from the stories of the victims and from the research of scholars, everything concerning the style no less than the sheer magnitude of the genocide, makes the holocaust something qualitatively different from the worst antisemitic visions generated in the past. The holocaust is a phenomenon *sui generis*.

And so, ironically, it is again less the understanding of the apocalypse experienced by the victims that is illuminated by the *Protocols* than the self-understanding of the persecutors, those whom Eric Hoffer called the "true believers," and their *Führer*. As the Allied and Russian armies ever more tightly encircled his bunker, which from the outside vaguely resembled a concentration camp with its barbed wire and line posts, Hitler alternated between temper tantrums and fits of melancholy. As his world crumbled around him, however, his increasingly deranged mind probably still sought an explanation for what had befallen him and his nation. Norman Cohn put it well when he wrote that "in this preposterous fabrication from the days of the Russian pogroms Hitler heard the call of a kindred spirit, and he responded to it with all his being."[53]

Hitler must have been proud of the response by his people to the danger posed by the Jews. Julius Streicher, whom the race traitors vilified as an obsessive and mentally unhinged psychopath, had loyally hammered home the existence of a worldwide Jewish conspiracy in issue after issue of his antisemitic *Der Sturmer*. In film, too, Fritz Hippler portrayed scenes that could have come straight from the *Protocols,* and he depicted the Jews as the filthy vermin that Hitler's racial specialists "proved" they were in *Der Ewige Jude* (1940). The *Führer* had even put Dr. Franz Alfred Six, his leading expert on Freemasonry,[54] in charge of Section VII of the Reich Security Head Office in 1939 in order to learn more about the conspiracy exposed in the *Protocols*. This scholar's heart was surely in the right place: Six enthusiastically endorsed the plan for the "physical elimination of Eastern Jewry" while participating at the Conference of Advisers on Jewish Matters in 1944 as a member of the Foreign Office. But what good did it do? His cultural apologists, Hitler must have thought, were no better than his generals.

Victory had been ripped from his grasp: how was it possible? The *Führer* was known to have cried again and again that the Germans were no longer worthy of him, that they had betrayed him, and that they deserved to die. But what had happened to them? What had led them to treason? Or, better, who? Perhaps Hitler was thinking of the *Protocols* when he ended his political testament with the words: "Above all, I demand of the nation's leaders and followers scrupulous adherence to the race laws and to ruthless resistance against the world poisoners of all peoples, international Jewry."[55]

Amid the drum roll of bombs and guns, psychological projection raged and he refused to acknowledge any mistakes. Hitler considered the logic of the *Protocols* his own: it was not he who had started the war or, if he had, then it was because the Jews had declared war on him. It was as it had always been since time immemorial. Those Jews were clever beasts: Ludendorff had already identified them with both the Freemasons and the Jesuits. The old fool may not have been much of a general, according to Hitler, but here he knew what he was talking about: the Jews were the mobilizing agents of progress, constantly willing to sacrifice the spiritual for the material, the experiential for the intellectual, and thus the longstanding enemy of Christian civilization and the Aryan race.

War with the Jews was unavoidable, an elemental fact of life, an eternal encounter. They had envisioned that a supranational empire could only be built on an intensified nationalism.[56] The *Protocols* saw "the ruins of the natural and genealogical aristocracy" that seemed to demand the creation of a new racial aristocracy, and it warned against any form of "blood poisoning." It was all there in the *Protocols* and, if not in the pamphlet, then in Chamberlain, or Wagner, or the other antisemites whose works surely blended in Hitler's mind. But now the Jews had won: Germany would, for the second time, suffer a "stab in the back."

How was it possible? Hitler knew what needed to be done. His plans to resettle the Jews in Madagascar or in Lapland or in Siberia were probably mere diversions. He had hunted them down, rooted them out of public life, burned down their synagogues, and ultimately annihilated six million of them in the camps. Still it was not enough. How could they have survived? Was it all explicable through racial analysis? Perhaps the *Protocols* intimated a better answer. The "antisemitism of reason" might also have its limits. The Jews must be in league with the devil. What other explanation made sense? He had only been doing God's work, Hitler must have thought, and now the devil's agents were taking their revenge—not merely upon the German people, too weak and too irresolute to resist them, and who therefore deserved the disaster in which they were now mired, but upon *him*.

Some among those he met looked into his eyes and saw nothing; others remarked upon the fire. But there was really no contradiction: hell is nothingness and hell burns. It was always the same, or so he must have thought. They all probably wondered why he should have again begun talking publicly about annihilating the Jews in 1939. They must have thought him pathological upon initiating the "final solution" in 1941, employing valuable resources and manpower to eliminate the damned race, just when the war was reaching its peak. But it all made perfect sense: the war was, beyond anything else Germany might gain, the way to solve the Jewish question. The annihilation of the nation's enemies, the antifascist alliance now controlled by Jews in Washington and Moscow, demanded the annihilation of European Jewry.

The *Protocols* had explained the conspiracy: Hitler was faced with a single enemy. Inside the *Reich* and arrayed against it from the outside were the Jews. *He* was the victim and not the Jews. His situation was no different than that of those who ran the concentration camps: they were the victims not the Jews since they had been called upon to commit the worst crime in history in order to save humanity from those they persecuted. The toll upon *him* had been inhuman. The others couldn't possibly know the burden he was bearing. In those last days, of course, he knew that they were conspiring against him. They undoubtedly were talking about how his face had the white pallor of death and how his hands were shaking. But he would show them: he would remain at his post until the very end changing the strategy of his generals and shifting around non-existent divisions in a battle already lost. Embittered and engulfed in self-pity, as Adolf Hitler put his gun into his mouth, he surely saw the wretched image of his enemy and thought: there is still so much to do.

The Legacy of a Lie:
Contemporary Antisemitism
and Its Future

*And, indeed, as he listened to the cries of joy rising from the town,
[he] remembered that such joy is always imperiled. He knew what
those jubilant crowds did not know but could have learned from
books: that the plague bacillus never dies or disappears for good;
that it can lie dormant for a years and years in furniture and linen
chests; that it bides its time in bedrooms, cellars, trunks, and
bookshelves; and that perhaps the day would come when, for the
bane and enlightening of men, it would rouse up its rats again and
send them forth to die in a happy city.*

—Albert Camus, *The Plague (1947)*

The Jewish conspiracy had triumphed: those antisemites who survived the war, the followers of the Nazis and the followers of their followers, surely felt there was even more to do. Former Nazis and officers of the SS escaped to Sweden, South America, and certain Arab states. They took with them their beliefs and the need to justify them anew. The *Protocols* undoubtedly remained in their hearts and there are those who still endorse the views articulated in the pamphlet.[1] They probably know nothing of the past. And, even if they do, what they know undoubtedly derives from neo-Nazis like David Irving and Fred Leuchter, tendentious authors like Ernst Nolte and Robert Faurisson, or "revisionist" journals like the *Historical Review*. All of them are intent only on mitigating the character of the holocaust and the nature of antisemitism.[2]

The spurious knowledge possessed by antisemites always leaves them steadfast in their prejudices. It enables them to resist logical correction or empirical refutation: Jean-Paul Sartre was correct when he remarked that antisemites turn themselves into stone. Justifications for their claims always have less to do with issues of truth than attempts to provide themselves with feelings of superiority they have done nothing to earn. This was certainly the case with the authors and advocates of the *Protocols*. They were never interested in genuine debate or social scientific findings: they identified truth with feeling because it freed them from using the intellect. Therein lies the broader existential attraction of a prejudice like antisemitism: it may sometimes appeal to intellectuals, but it always indulges the idiot.

The *Protocols* was written for the idiot. It expresses the vulgarity of racism and the violence endemic, if often hidden, within antisemitism. The pamphlet was a forgery and a pack of lies; there was never anything authentic about it. For many living in our "postmodern condition,"[3] however, this is essentially irrelevant: their relativism leads them to question the very notion of evidence in judging truth claims. One interpretive position is as good, or bad, as any other and there exist an infinite number of ways to interpret any given text. Paranoia can, in this vein, become a legitimate response to the "hyper-real" quality of modern life and its fragmentary character. Certain thinkers have even claimed that the belief in alien abduction should be taken seriously if only because it is an innovative way of constructing a perspective through which people can express their experiences.[4] According to this kind of logic, of course, the paranoid claims of the *Protocols*, arguably *the* canonical text in the history of conspiracy theory, must be taken seriously as well.

There should be no misunderstanding: unless antisemitism is seen as a worldview, with its own logic and premises, coming to grips with it becomes infinitely more difficult. Ideological phenomena with mass appeal must be analyzed with great care in terms of their sociological implications. But this does not mean that the truth-claims made by these ideologies or their views about the workings of reality must be taken as legitimate in their own right. Without criteria for justification or falsification there is simply no need to be skeptical about beliefs regarding the mortal threat posed by a "secret" alliance of international bankers, liberal politicians, space aliens, and the Antichrist.[5] Criticism of any work of political theory depends upon the ability to draw lines, no matter how blurry, between fact and falsehood or authenticity and inauthenticity, consistency and tautology. Some objective referent is necessary for making judgments, and the basic assumptions underpinning common notions of legal, scholarly, and historical evidence have not outlived their usefulness. There is no substitute for an open dialogue, a willingness to deal with genuine criticism, or an ability to justify claims by making reference to empirical reality.

Personal experience is an unreliable guide when dealing with truth-claims because, whether consciously or unconsciously, ideology and fantasy often impinge upon it. Where all forms of objectivity are called into question, and all categories of judgment become equally arbitrary, there is no need to justify anything. Nothing then qualifies as truth and everything appears as an "artificial social construct." Under these circumstances, the *Protocols* becomes just another work, no different in terms of its truth content than *The Politics* of Aristotle or a great novel. It becomes a work, like all works, of "fiction."

A postmodern perspective of this sort rips works from their historical contexts and intellectual traditions. It ignores the original intent inspiring the creation of the work, the social functions it performs, and the political impact it evidences in historical struggles. The forgers of the *Protocols* knew what they were doing. The pamphlet was created with an eye toward furthering the political fight for a certain kind of world. Perhaps it is true that the *Protocols* inspired a few great literary figures, and ubiquitous fears of a Jewish conspiracy may even have perversely mitigated the introduction of antisemitic policies in Japan.[6] But the exceptions do not invalidate

the rule. The multiplicity of *possible* literary interpretations is qualified by the rather narrow ways in which the pamphlet *has been*
interpreted. There are reasons why, overwhelmingly, the political
right rather than the left should have embraced the *Protocols.*

The *Protocols* is not a work of "fiction" that infuses reality with
fantasy and highlights the repressed moments of freedom. It instead
treats fantasy as reality, the experience of the subject as objective. The
pamphlet constrains the imagination, and it brooks no opposition to
the prejudices informing it. Its interests become its truths by *fiat:* the
work remains a *lie,* a subversion of discourse, a glorification of "hate-
speech."[7] This indeed has led some to suggest, almost in triumphal
tones and without any sense of what this would involve, placing a ban
on the *Protocols.*[8]

Freedom of speech is a complex issue: it is the subject of
countless works and untold debates. At the risk of simplifying,
however, calls for censorship are usually predicated on a sense of
moral injury. The situation is compounded with the *Protocols* since
it served as an incitement for real violence against Jews. The
mistake of the Swiss Court of Appeals was less in stating that the
pamphlet was a not work of "smut literature" than in refusing to
deal with what was really at stake. Whether to ban antisemitic and
racist texts of this sort rests on a *political* judgment: does the moral
offense offered by the work far outweigh the insights it might
provide and, what amounts to the same thing, does its publication
actually constitute a clear and present danger to liberal society and
its Jewish citizens?

The Jew may once have been the pariah. But the blatant
discrimination of times past, experienced in virtually every facet of
everyday life, has essentially been abolished. The issue is not
whether at the United Nations or in Paris or Hong Kong this or
that sophisticated individual approvingly referred to the *Protocols,*
whether some retrograde sect or antisemitic official sought to use it
for political gain, or whether some small publisher in Boston or
London brought out a new edition.[9] Concerns over the threat
posed by antisemitism cannot simply rest on whether this or that
African-American politician spoke about an "amen corner" for the

support of Israel by the United States, whether a political activist described New York as "hymie-town," or even whether support for Israel is becoming more qualified. None of this speaks to the pressing danger of antisemitism in the contemporary world. Things can always change. Nevertheless, for the moment, it would be difficult to identify a serious *political* threat to Jewish life in the western democracies.[10]

Antisemitism has become like background noise, an incessant and irritating hum, that should not be mistaken for the real music. The ideology of hate still has a certain appeal at the fringes of political life and among thousands upon thousands of discontented individuals. Refusing to endorse the need for censorship does not mean that progressive booksellers must sell the *Protocols* in their bookstores or that liberal magazines should accept ads from the publishers of the pamphlet. The liberal mind militates against the sensibility of a work like the *Protocols*. Its salience for a liberal society exists only in its clarification of those prejudices underpinning the *illiberal* alternative.

Genuine democratic education calls upon citizens to make decisions not only about what they want but also about what they need to know. Santayana's famous truism, that those who forget history are condemned to repeat it, is probably not quite as true as many would care to believe. But the contemporary public still needs to understand what inspired the imagination of Nazism and other antisemitic movements all over the world. They deserve to see what informs the authoritarian personality. The work of the progressive critic begins with illuminating the unintended consequences of fabricated appeals to prejudice. This requires support for liberal political values rather than a knee-jerk response in favor of repression. Dealing with falsehood is an immanent moment in arriving at truth, and coming to terms with the past means facing the evil it unleashed. There is nothing safe about freedom.

There are times, of course, when even a liberal society will find the need for political censorship unavoidable: the early and late years of the Weimar Republic, when right-wing extremism presented a tangible threat to its existence, was arguably such a time. Perhaps in the Russia of today and in certain other states of Eastern Europe, where antisemitism is on the rise and republican values have not yet taken root, it is also possible to make claims for censorship. There is a pragmatic matter, however, which is rarely considered by those advocating censorship of works like the *Protocols*. It is always easier for republican regimes to engage in censorship when there is *no* real threat to its existence, or to certain of its citizens, than when such a threat actually exists.

Antisemitism also does not simply disappear when its ideological expressions are prohibited. If inflammatory pamphlets are summarily banned, not only will antisemitic and racist prejudices fester, but those sitting on the fence will have cause to wonder about the liberality of their own liberal regime. Censorship inherently exhibits the lack of faith in what Jürgen Habermas has appropriately called "constitutional patriotism." Repression is never a virtue, but rather— at best—a necessity. The lessons of history are unambiguous on this point: whenever necessity has been extolled as a virtue, the result has always been self-delusion and worse.

THE *PROTOCOLS* IN OUR TIME

The world is different than it was in the interwar period: antisemitism is no longer either an ideology dealing with the destiny of mankind or a pretext.[11] The dialectical implications deriving from the defeat of Hitler have, moreover, still not been fully appreciated. The overwhelming attempt to destroy the Jews turned into its opposite: the holocaust left in its wake a Jewish people more existentially, if not necessarily politically, unified than ever before. The destruction of fascism initiated what has become a strengthened commitment to the values of the liberal state; it also transformed the labor movement, the longstanding enemy of traditional elites. The new political landscape ushered in a set of new social movements intent on highlighting the repression of the *other*. Hitler's defeat robbed western antisemites of the prerequisites for political victory: it stripped them of their legitimacy, destroyed their symbols, elevated their racial enemies, and left them without a viable institutional alternative to the liberal state.

The Nazis ultimately produced what they wished to abolish: the sacrifice of a generation on the slaughter bench of history created a new form of solidarity among Jews, whatever their current religious and political differences, and also a profound sympathy for their suffering among many gentiles. Past ethnic and religious divisions among Jews pale in comparison with the general agreement on the slogan: "Never again!" There are, of course, limits to all of this. Fundamental rifts between the orthodox and reformist wings of the Jewish community have resurfaced with great bitterness in Israel. Although the more liberal elements in German society have attempted to "work through the past" (*Vergangenheitsbewältigung*), such an undertaking has been less forceful in other nations like Austria, France, and in much of Eastern Europe. Even in most of these countries, however, Jewish organizations inspired by the experiences of an antisemitic past, and fearful of their reoccurrence, have been able to organize forthrightly and openly in defense of Jewish rights and interests with new vigor.[12] Liberal states also no longer suffer the same lack of legitimacy as their predecessors of the interwar period. Antisemitism has lost its status as a legitimate political position and it has become unacceptable in most arenas of public life in the West.

The marginalization of the antisemite is connected with Hitler's greatest success: the destruction of the radical labor movement in both its socialist and communist variants. Since its successors no longer pose a threat to capitalism or its elites, or at least not in the manner of times past, the idea of a Jewish world conspiracy carried out by the Reds has lost all credibility. Outside the Arab world, the view of "Jewish" capital has changed as well: the new technology and new mobility of capital, its computers and radically expanded forms of information resources, are increasingly opening each individual to the world of others living very different lives. Current attempts to identify Jews with the workings of international capital and international organizations are pathetic responses to new global economic policies intertwined with the inclusion of the *other* and the growth of a new cosmopolitan sensibility. The Jew is no longer regarded as the absolute enemy, and the fear of Jews has lost its resonance among the general public.

The *Protocols* have been driven underground. Its appeal remains only for those intent on fostering authoritarian nationalism, exorcising the terrors of modernization, and reacting against the march of secularism. Nine Arabic editions of the tract were printed between 1951 and 1971.[13] Nasser employed the tract cynically in Egypt during his dictatorial reign, which began in the 1950s, and in 1984 various sections of it appeared in the Iranian journal, *Imam*. Other nations like Libya, Saudi Arabia, and Tunisia also publicized the *Protocols* as a tool in their ongoing struggles with Israel.[14] Idi Amin embraced the pamphlet during his murderous reign in Uganda and various Japanese authors turned it into a cult favorite during the 1980s. New editions have appeared in small runs in Pakistan and Malaysia as well as a number of important nations in South America. Two thousand copies of the *Protocols* were published in Croatia during 1996 and it has also surfaced elsewhere in the Balkans. Pamyat and other right-wing groups, which generally receive more publicity than their numbers justify, regularly refer to it in the new Russia. Even in these nations, however, it no longer plays anything like the role it played in times past.

With respect to the United States, speaking politically and ideologically, antisemitism lacks any genuine mass appeal. The National States Rights Party and the California Noontide Press distributed the *Protocols* during the 1970s and it is still hailed by representatives of the right-wing militias: Norman Phillips, author of the neofascist best-seller *The Turner Diaries,* for example, identified the American state as a "Zionist Occupation Government." The *Protocols* is openly sold on the streets of the larger American cities by followers of the Nation of Islam. Jerry Falwell announced on January 14, 1999 that the Antichrist is alive and undoubtedly a male Jew; other respectable leaders of the Christian Coalition refer to the *Protocols'* themes at their rallies before making their obligatory retraction. The pamphlet is taken seriously by the Christian Defence League and members of other extreme fundamentalist groups like Smyrna. Its arguments are also promulgated by tiny Aryan sects and the paranoiacs associated with Lyndon LaRouche, the John Birch Society, and the Liberty Lobby. Nevertheless, this only confirms the irrelevance of the *Protocols* for the intellectual and political main-stream of American life.

The brochure has become the possession of cranks, fringe movements, and outlaw states. Its advocates, however, have a new outlet: the Internet.[15] Just as the initial success of the *Protocols* derived from the need for dislocated groups and individuals to explain the impact of modernity upon them, which involved blaming its delete-rious effects on outsiders like the Jews, the new postmodern society in this current *fin de siècle* generates questions for which antisemitism provides illusory answers. According to a specific subject search on Altavista in 1999, there were over 9000 listed sites pertaining specifically to the *Protocols,* close to 60,000 dealing with antisemit-ism, over 135,000 related to the Illuminati, and more than 126,000 concerned with conspiracy theories. Not all of these worldwide sites, of course, are antisemitic or provide a positive image of the *Protocols.* Many like the Hate Page of the Week or the Net Hate Page are sharply critical and important participants in the contemporary struggle against the resurgence of fascist ideas.[16] But there are more than enough antisemitic sites to suggest that the Internet has given the *Protocols* a new profile. Indeed, it is becoming increasingly evident that the new forms of paranoid conspiracy theory bear

> . . . a striking resemblance to antisemitic propaganda manufactured in pre–World War II Germany, with only the slight obfuscation of substituting "international bankers" for Jews. . . . Somehow these tales—once suggested—inflame the fears and paranoia of people to the extent that even when the Jewish target is "removed" . . . a residue remains in the human imagination that is happy to attach itself to a more vague target. For let us admit that many people positively enjoy being in such "snits" of paranoia, bogus "insight," fear, discontent-ment, etc. that propaganda like this evokes . . . [and] we do not have to even be openly antisemitic to enjoy these effects."[17]

The *Protocols* still exhibits its appeal. But it does so in a new way: the medium has indeed become the message. The Internet serves as the postmodern substitute for the political leaflet. It is uncensored, unapologetic, and wholly anarchic; it is also instant, international, and cheap. Virtually all the marginal fascist parties and organizations in western Europe have a home page: the list includes the British National Party, the Front National in France, the Alleanza Nazionale in Italy, the Vlams Blok in Belgium, and the largest computer network in Germany called, interestingly enough, the Thule Network. The *Protocols* thrives in cyberspace.

But the Internet isolates even as it unifies. It atomizes even as it coordinates. If individuals on the fringe often employ the Internet *anonymously* to advocate their views, its use by extremist groups actually helps antifascists and humanists track them and their activities. Rarely pointed out is the fact that

> those monitoring racism and antisemitism have a new intelligence source that was simply not there before. The fact that racists and antisemites have embraced the Internet with such zeal has made the task of keeping up with them easier. Moreover, it has been of very specific use in official action against extremists. . . . Although the Internet is seen as free, and anarchic, and beyond control, nevertheless, the presence of the racists could be seen as an unwitting form of self-imposed social control, both because of the conventions they have to adhere to and the fact that they can be monitored. If 'battles' with them are fought out on the Net rather than in the streets, that constitutes an interesting development.[18]

Prejudice is always in *reserve:* there is still real antisemitic feeling even if the possibilities for its organized expression have changed. Antisemitism lurks beneath the surface of events in much the same way as the supposed conspiracy that its advocates projected upon the Jews. It still "thrives on archetypal fears, anxieties, and reflexes that seem to defy any rational analysis."[19] The present danger should not be ignored, in short, even if it should not be exaggerated. Because so many people refer to a secret conspiracy, especially under postmodern conditions in which the need for evidence is being increasingly relativized, its existence can easily be taken for granted. What distinguishes the radically paranoid style of works like the *Protocols,* however, is not belief in this or that conspiracy by this or that group: it is rather the belief that history *itself* is a conspiracy forged by a single all-powerful and transcendent force whose defeat is dependent upon an unremitting crusade.[20] This view is simply no longer relevant even for the majority of antisemites.

Western antisemitism has taken on a *free-floating* form. It no longer has the distinct characteristics of the past. The fine-tuned justifications are gone. Sectarian religious fanatics might still wish to save the individual by calling for the conversion of the Jew; but these groups lack the force of public opinion and coercive political institutions like the medieval church. In a similar fashion, while *rishes,* or social prejudice, against Jews obviously still exists, there are no serious proposals on the table for shoving the Jews back into a ghetto or restricting their access to the manifold institutions of public life. Given the symbolic impact of the holocaust, moreover, the idea of denying the Jew as both a Jew and a person has lost its appeal. It is no longer fashionable to identify Jews with a subhuman race and antisemitism lacks "respectable" thinkers such as Barrès or Chamberlain. The new free-floating antisemitism, lacking any new forms or means of justification, is a hodgepodge of ad hoc claims.

This crisis in antisemitic theory is reflected in antisemitic practice. None of the existing fringe organizations is even remotely capable of realizing what might be termed the universal aims of antisemitism. Few any longer concern themselves with "proving" the authenticity of the *Protocols.*[21] Antisemitism has lost its connection with the uniforms and ensignia, the pogroms and riots, the coordinated propaganda and the academically reinforced dogma, the disciplined *ligues* and authoritarian parties intent upon making a serious political assault upon the state. The ideology has become detached from the interests of any particular class or mass movement genuinely competing for political power in the West.

Kept alive by tiny sects in the insular world of sectarian politics, groups incapable of conceptualizing the workings of the "hidden hand" upon civilization as a whole, antisemitism has become little more than a breathing corpse. Its proponents vent their anger against the dynamics of modernity which, due to their own premodern prejudices, they cannot possibly comprehend. Embracing the most vulgar product of a general climate built on suspicion, prizing the irrational over the rational, they simply *believe* they can forge their own conspiracy to defend against the "Jewish" new world order, with its interventionist state no less than its diverse social movements intent on expanding the realm of subjective experience and letting a new form of pluralism unfold. These new antisemites still reveal the latent violence behind what Nietzsche initially considered a psychological form of "resentment." Their fears about an increasingly cosmopolitan civilization and its supposed harbingers, the Jews, leads them to constrain their own intellects and deny their own potential. They close themselves off from the world. Indeed, for this very reason, the battle against antisemitism remains a struggle against *a way of thinking* in which rumors about the Jews are the only necessary proof of their own validity.

THE LOSERS

Antisemitism is the stupid answer to a serious question: how does history operate behind our backs? Adam Smith saw an "invisible hand" coordinating individual self-interest with the common good, balancing supply and demand, under capitalism; Hegel explained the way in which the "cunning of reason" *(List der Vernunft)* uses individuals by turning the consequences of their actions against their intentions. Marx believed that people make their own history, but "not as they please":[22] he saw capitalism as unintentionally producing its proletarian "gravediggers" while eliminating all premodern classes in the process.[23] The *Protocols* provides a more pessimistic, simpler, and more dramatic response to concerns of this sort. It offers no evidence for its empirical claims and it is incapable of understanding the structure of social systems. It also has no room for ambiguity, ambivalence, or dialectics. Its persuasive power derives from its ability to deduce everything from a single proposition. The most terrible unintended consequences of social action are not unintentional at all: "the hidden hand" of the Jews manipulates everything.

This antisemitic message has traditionally been more persuasive for some groups than others. In the 1920s it appealed to war veterans, incapable of dealing with civilian life or making sense of the apocalypse they had just barely survived, along with youths of good upbringing stripped of their prospects for a decent life. But the most receptive audience for antisemitic ideology has generally been the stalwarts of the provincial community (*Gemeinschaft*): aristocrats incapable of realizing that their time is past, the peasantry and the small shopkeepers, the low-level bureaucrats and the dregs of the industrial metropolis (*Gesellschaft*). There were the *Lumpenproletarians*, insecure academics, paranoid fanatics, and even unemployed workers without knowledge or hope. These groups constituted the mass base for European fascism and many of them still serve as core clientele for the Nation of Islam, the KKK, and the militias in the United States. They are the losers left behind by modernity. Their plight demands explanation and their resentment needs confirmation: this is what works like the *Protocols* provide.

Antisemitism in particular and conspiracy theories in general make complex historical patterns comprehensible by their oversimplification. Such ideologies claim to identify the underlying or hidden source of human misery. They also claim to make this source concrete whether in the person of the Jew or the image of a "new world order" and thereby, strangely enough, empower those seeking to resist. Opposition to the arguments offered by conspiracy theory is always seen as controlled or dictated, whether consciously or unconsciously, by the cabal. That they are not taken seriously by the broader public, moreover, justifies the rage of the losers. It also absolves them of responsibility for events. They have done their duty: they have heroically provided the warning against the machinations of a ruthless and all-powerful enemy.

Conspiracy theories serve important social functions and fill various psychological needs: they are as deserving of serious *critical* study as any number of other religious, social, or political beliefs.[24] Understanding the popular reception of the *Protocols* is impossible without making reference to the way that modernity is experienced by those whose material existence and existential self-identification are both threatened by it. The losers fear the modern production process, its dominant ideologies of liberalism and socialism, and its dominant classes, the bourgeoisie and the working class. A small farmer in a small town or an aristocrat or a member of the "middle strata *(Mittlestand)*, for example, would *most likely* reject the politics of both the labor movement and the bourgeoisie. He would most likely fear the former for its attempts to impinge upon his property as surely as the latter for its control of his mortgage. It would make as little sense for him to embrace historical materialism, which sees his class as doomed, as a form of liberalism contemptuous of "community" and committed to cosmopolitanism values. This small farmer will most likely, if obviously not always, lash out against industrialization and all philosophies resting on a commitment to progress. Even in modern society, what Max Weber termed an "elective affinity" exists between particular ideologies and particular social groups.[25]

Capitalism develops in a complicated relation with the remnants of precapitalist classes and modernity retains within itself, sometimes even invigorates, the premodern.[26] The new society generates an anxiety, tantamount to what Sartre has termed an "objective neurosis," among the losers or those who believe they will become losers. This neurosis is not some metapsychological expression of the collective unconscious or some national cultural predisposition. It derives instead from the concrete experience of modernity undergone by the losers who will not go softly into the night but, instead, rage against it.

Older classes like the peasantry and the aristocracy are undoubtedly passing away and their values lack resonance in advanced industrial society. But their fears are now the fears of those who have lost faith in the ability of progressive forces to deal with the problems of modern life. Under the proper circumstances, indeed, these fears can intensify among the losers or, perhaps even more importantly, those who believe they will become the losers in the conflicts generated by modernity. Fears will then turn into anxieties or even neuroses. These manifest themselves among individuals and groups in an ever stronger insecurity of self-definition, a feeling of worthlessness, a sense of irrelevance, or what might be termed an *identity deficit*.

Such sentiments grow in periods of crisis and, with them, often the allure of antisemitism. This ideology compensates the losers, or those who believe they will become losers, for the deficit they feel in their own lives. It becomes a way of explaining why history has passed them by. It enables them to place responsibility upon others for their diminished status and thereby fosters the need for a scapegoat. The logic provided by antisemitism is implacable. Its adherent indeed "chooses the irremediable out of fear of being free; he chooses mediocrity out of fear of being alone, and out of pride he makes of this irremediable mediocrity a rigid aristocracy. To this end he finds the existence of the Jew absolutely necessary. Otherwise to whom would he feel superior?"[27]

Antisemitism suggests that failure was *never* the fault of the loser. Conspiracy theory makes it possible to believe that the given crisis has been artificially created by an all-powerful "alien entity," a subversive clique, operating in the body politic for its own purposes. It thereby affirms the intelligence of the loser. The conspiratorial worldview "leaves no room for mistakes, failures, or ambiguities."[28] It provides certainty. The prominence of works like the *Protocols* is consequently dependent upon the degree of uncertainty caused by the given crisis. The deeper the crisis, the more it will make possible the mobilization of hitherto untouched masses, and the more scapegoating ideologies will take the form of a "contagion."[29]

Antisemitism always retains the potential of becoming *total* in its view of the Jew.[30] The *other* of civilization, who is also so fully implicated in its development, becomes the source of *all* its economic, social, and political problems. The success of the antisemitic enterprise subsequently depends upon the ability to portray the enemy as the *total* incarnation of evil. Only insofar as this task is accomplished can antisemitic ideology explode the ethnic, racial, and class barriers separating its proponents from one another. It only follows, in keeping with the insight of Hannah Arendt, that antisemitism should prove strongest where the Jew is visible without enjoying real power or "just visible enough." The total crisis caused by the total enemy always, even if only implicitly, suggests the need for an equally total response to the "Jewish question."

It is a different matter with other forms of prejudice. Racists consider blacks inherently inferior to whites and a drain on public finances, but they don't simultaneously claim that people of color control capital and the media. English racism depicted the Irish as dirty, lazy, and apelike, but its proponents never believed that the Irish were manipulating the British Empire. The situation is similar when it comes to the ways that sexists view women or the ways that homophobes consider gays. Other forms of prejudice stereotype their enemy with fixed qualities: they are stupid, they are hurtful, and they can serve a distinct political purpose. Nevertheless, the prejudice exhibited by other types of bigots is inherently *partial* and therein lies its limits.

Antisemitism has no limits. It is predicated less on attributing fixed qualities, even when it comes to stereotypical images of the misanthropic miser or slimy social climber, than letting the Jew appear in *all* guises. The Jew is the capitalist *and* the communist, the avant-garde artist *and* the provincial pawnbroker, the pacifist *and* the belligerent; the Jew is both visible and invisible, assimilated and unassimilated, aboveground and underground. The Jew can be anywhere and anyone. It is as if

> an endlessly changing and endlessly mimetic force had launched a constantly shifting offensive against humanity. . . . [T]he all-pervasive threat becomes in fact formless and unrepresentable; as such it leads to the most frightening phantasm of all: a threat that looms everywhere, that, although it penetrates everything, is an invisible carrier of death, like poison gas spreading over the battlefields of the Great War.[31]

The indeterminacy of the Jew is what makes him or her so dangerous, so creative of anxiety, for the antisemite. Are the Jews equivalent to a race, a culture, a religion, a nation, or an economic system? It's impossible to decide: the *other* must encompass all these definitions and, for this reason, the material interests and intellectual messages of the Jews must be in constant flux. This indeterminacy allows the antisemite to *fit* the Jew into any context, to change stereotypes in the blink of an eye, and to find the source of any problem. The antisemite turns the Jew into a *chameleon*. Thus, an unwavering critic of the *Protocols* could write:

> Every country has Jews, every country has evils: therefore the Jews are the cause of the evils. Such is the crude logic of demos and demagogues. Even the better political parties of our country need a whipping-boy to explain their defeat at the polls. The Jews are as good as a foreign war in averting attention from the financial scandals caused by the unethical and unscrupulous manipulations of leading financiers and infinitely more economical. Is it profiteering that agitates the public? It is the Jews who are the profiteers. Is it the menace of Bolshevism? They are the Bolshevists. Is it the hidden hand? That hand wears heavy Jewish rings. Is it a shortage of houses? It is the Jews who have monopolized all accommodation. Is it a dearth of bacon? It is the Jews who have eaten it up. Is it the awful consequences of imperialistic ambition? The Kaiser has Jewish blood. Is it the country suffering from a too ambitious form of clericalism? The Pope is a successor of Peter and he was a Jew. If there were no Jews, they would have to be invented. . . . They are indispensable— the antithesis of a panacea; guaranteed to *cause* all evils.[32]

The explanatory power of antisemitism ultimately rests on its use of what might be termed the *chameleon-effect*. This fundamental element of its popular appeal in the past, however, is precisely what undermines its salience for the present. Antisemites may still rail on the Internet about the dangers of the hidden hand manipulating a host of forces. But there is no longer a core to their thinking. The problem is palpable no matter the number of hits on antisemitic web sites. The basic category is no longer applicable. The Jew is now no more or less a chameleon than anyone else. The chameleon effect has become generalized among the populace at large. The real gentile can now live like the fictional Jew.

No longer are most people chained to the occupations of their parents, the town in which they were born, the lifelong marriage, the church of their community, and the straight heterosexual life style. It is simply counterintuitive when paranoiac antisemites claim:

> The powers that govern would have all armies under one head, all money would be the same, all people would be totally dependent on this new force or perish. There would only be one nice, accepting religion allowed (to keep people from saying nasty things to each other and causing them to feel guilty) and there would be one king in all the earth. Of course, the new power would get everyone together and let them vote that all of this would be okay. They would vote for it because no one wants to get all shot up.[33]

Each now increasingly has the opportunity of forging his or her own "biography" and becoming a chameleon in his or her own life. There is no longer a fixed all-embracing *other* because there is no longer a fixed all-embracing self.[34] The explanation for the diminished status of antisemitism in advanced industrial society, its nebulous quality, is not simply political in nature. It is also not merely a function of more "information," which T. S. Eliot liked to differentiate from "knowledge," or a plethora of interest groups. It is rather that more people are increasingly experiencing a more varied and yet more intensive form of multicultural education. Indeed, beyond the odious expressions of intolerance by this ethnic or that racial organization, education of this sort is fostering an ever greater reliance upon cosmopolitan values and tolerance in the everyday life of democratic societies.

Antisemites are unaware of how the absolutism of their prejudice marginalizes them. They are trapped in the world of the *Protocols:* fixed, paranoiac, and dominated by myth. Those who should actually seek a critical understanding of it are, ironically, less the Jews than the antisemites. But they can't. They are the victims of a self-chosen blindness. These *true believers* have cast their lot with the irrational, the dogmatic, and the provincial. They span the globe. There are the rabble-rousers in western Europe, explicitly anti-immigrant and implicitly antisemitic, lacking a program while searching for a scapegoat. There are the authoritarian reactionaries in the former Soviet Union seeking a return to the traditions of old and the communists, seduced by nationalism but too cowardly to contest a burgeoning antisemitism. There are the Islamic fundamentalists still incapable of analyzing Israeli policies without reference to an international Jewish conspiracy. And there are other *believers* closer to home. There are the nationalists among people of color who cite the *Protocols* to justify their belief that Jews ran the slave trade, control the banks, and hold down their constituencies.[35] There are the Baptist sects still committed to converting the Jews, the Catholics still harboring their hatred of the Christ-killers, as well as the establishmentarian conservatives and the guilty liberals unwilling to offend their more prejudiced allies. The *Protocols* belongs to all of them. It is *their* story and "working through" the past, *their* past, is ultimately *their* responsibility.

THE VANISHING JEW

Questions remain: if antisemitism is no longer a threat in the terms of times past, what does this imply for Jews and for Judaism? It should have become clear by now that the *Protocols* was directed not simply against Jews, but rather the progressive political legacy of the Enlightenment and modernity in general. The pamphlet looks back with nostalgia to a world of theocracy and monarchs, uniformity and hierarchy, certainty and organic community. It is informed by political intolerance, religious dogmatism, and cultural provincialism. When faced with the challenges of modernity in the next century, whether wittingly or unwittingly, will Jews embrace the same values in order to maintain their religious traditions and their unique sense of identity?

Liberal society may have lifted discriminatory barriers and it may have guaranteed civil liberties. It may have constrained the arbitrary exercise of political power and it may have inhibited intolerance. But it is one thing, after all, to reject the unwarranted prejudice directed against one's own group: it is quite another to extend political tolerance, religious pluralism, and cosmopolitanism to other groups or even dissidents within one's own group.

Many Jews are indeed wary of genuinely embracing the values denied by antisemitic tracts like the *Protocols*. Enough believe that, for all its benefits, liberal society has undermined the need for Jews to identify with one another, preserve their rituals, maintain their community, and perhaps even realize their "destiny." Its individualism seemingly subverts tradition, its secularism contests religious faith, its rationalism confronts ritual, and its universalism threatens what has been called the "inner survival" of American Jewry.[36] Might the liberal society yet prove successful where totalitarianism failed? Might the *disappearance of antisemitism* ultimately bring about the *disappearance of the Jews?*

Fears over the vanishing Jew have created allies between religious fundamentalists and ultranationalists within the Jewish community.[37] It is true that the connections between them are fraught with tenisons. Unfortunately, however, these groups and tendencies have increasingly been overshadowed by an eschatological orthodoxy and an expansionist xenophobic Zionism united in their contempt for the constitutional state and modern multicultural society.

The religious see the growing indifference among so many of their brethren to Jewish rituals and Jewish law, and the growth of reform Judaism as producing little more than the slow death of what had been an all-encompassing faith. It has also become increasingly difficult to maintain that the basic problems of Jewish identity derive from the diaspora and, in the manner of the ultranationalists, that uncritical identification with Israel and the unique "destiny" of the Jews offers a solution. Even various liberal intellectuals with a certain nostalgia for the past have recently begun worrying about the effects of intermarriage and the decline of ritual. Some speak about the need to rediscover a "Jewish state of mind."[38] Others highlight the "chosenness" of the Jews, the need to develop a Jewish "core curriculum" for interested adults, and the importance of "caring much more than we have."[39] These ideas are soft compared with those of the zealots. Implicitly or explicitly, however, they are all tinged with provincial assumptions. Such thinking can take a genuinely reactionary form when, with a glaring lack of sensitivity for those of other faiths, sociological problems are confronted by referring to those parts of the Scriptures where the survival of the Jews is assured because their "true purpose" is "to serve as God's people upon whom the redemption of God's world and God's own name uniquely depends."[40]

Progress has surely left an existential emptiness in its wake. The world is still a vale of tears. Issues of conscience, salvation, and meaning have arguably grown ever more pressing. Secularism wavers in the face of the lingering sickness, death, and what if anything comes afterward. Securing a sense of identity can help deal with issues of belonging and self-definition in a time of alienation and superficial consumerism: it can serve to counter the more spiritually debilitating elements of modern culture by strengthening what Edmund Burke considered a pact between "the dead, the living, and the yet unborn." The pressures of modernity have only intensified the need for answers to a host of questions concerning the meaning of life, mortality, and what existentialists liked to call "the extreme situation." No form of politics and no set of purely institutional arrangements can ever deal with such questions to the satisfaction of everyone or even most people.

A longing for certainty and security exhibits itself in contemporary life: fundamentalism has become a planetary phenomenon and, whatever the trends toward internationalism and cosmopolitanism the prospect of a world composed of ethnic ghettoes is real enough. It is still a matter of religious and nationalist zealots attempting to impose upon society their own particular notion of the good life. They still militate not merely against the *other*, the Arab or the Jew or the Christian, but also against the threat posed by the adherents of Enlightenment values within their own communities. The growing uncertainty associated with what *must* be certain, the trembling of nationalist convictions and religious faith only intensifies their commitment.

It is far more convenient for the preachers of conformity to blame larger social forces for their problems than to look in the mirror. The dangers posed by liberal society are the same dangers always posed by freedom: organized religion can no longer simply *assert* the social utility or ethical value of its dogma and *command* obedience. The proponents of orthodoxy can try to organize the political and existential needs of those whom progress leaves behind. But they can no longer take the truth of their belief as self-evident for *others*. The situation is no different for their secular counterparts: ultranationalists can no longer presume that their understanding of solidarity is valid for all members of the community. The resentment felt by fundamentalists and ultranationalists is all too palpable. It only makes sense that they should fear a new form of modernity in which religious dogma no less than cultural traditions must increasingly *prove* their relevance in a secular world of expanding opportunities for self-realization and an ever wider range of temptations. It is the same fear of modernity, *mutatis mutandis,* expressed by the *Protocols*.

But, still, the new authoritarians have framed the issue incorrectly. The issue is not the looming elimination of religion or "Jewishness" but rather a profound change in the tangible meaning of such notions. God and the religious community will not disappear. Organizational interests dictate that religious institutions, Jewish and non-Jewish alike, will seek to perpetuate themselves. But the character of these institutions and perhaps even the understanding of God are in the process of changing. It is now possible for ordinary people to pick and choose the rituals they will keep, the ethical guidelines they will embrace, and the spiritual claims they will believe. Ever less will these choices be made from fear of being stigmatized as a heretic by the community or the congregation. Religion is becoming an increasingly loose regulative framework for belief while God, perhaps in the manner best described by Martin Buber,[41] is ever more surely being seen as a personal referent offering comfort, self-examination, and perhaps even an inspiration for living uprightly.

The surfeit of contemporary zealotry is a reactionary response to the new religious possibilities offered by liberal society and the new hybrid cultures resulting from globalization. The intolerance of the zealots derives from their own real, if suppressed, doubts about whether their beliefs can still reach beyond their traditional congregations and provide meaningful answers to various questions dealing with the human condition. The new pluralism must seem nothing less than a slap in the face to the guardians of orthodoxy. They feel that no compromise is possible. Thus, ironically, the most likely source for a new antisemitism is the same as for a new authoritarian Judaism: movements intent on resisting the liberal state and cosmopolitan values while charging their religious faith with the pursuit of national, racial, or ethnic aims.

Perhaps the genuine message of the Torah calls for an assault on egoism and particularism in the name of caring for the weak, helping the stranger, and respecting the other; it might well demand "a reversal in the order of things."[42] But that is a challenge too few are willing to accept. Orthodox and ultranationalist sects embrace a special Jewish "destiny." Where the former refuse to consider their religion as one among many, the latter refuse to consider Israel as one state among others. The zealots fear not only a conspiracy among their Arab neighbors, which is in accord with the hatred they themselves project, but also a fundamental indifference to the plight of Jews by all gentile nations. They consider the current conflict between Israel and the Arab states as only the most recent episode in an ongoing conflict between Jews and the forces of evil.[43] They divide the world into Jews and "goys," us and them, the righteous and the profane. Religious dogmatism, social intolerance, and political prejudice are indeed not solely the province of antisemities: they also exist among certain Jews.

Democratic principles are irrelevant if they don't benefit them. The language used by ultraorthodox rabbis to condemn the judges of the Supreme Court and those who decided in 1999 to vote in favor of a Constitution for Israel is symptomatic and in keeping with the language of the *Protocols:* enemies are denounced as "wicked," "wanton," and "unclean." It is no different with those ultranationalists who dream of a new Jewish "people's community" *(Volksgemeinschaft)* and those who harbor imperialist ambitions: they resent a multicultural world in which the fading memory of six million dead is ever less sufficient to win a debate or justify a misguided state policy. They employ faith and historical memory as shields to absolve them from justifying their politics or dealing with their opponents in a reasonable fashion.

That is their right in the private sphere. But it is another matter in the public realm. The rabbi can prove as dogmatic as the priest. Separation of church and state is a bedrock for the maintenance of all other civil liberties. It is what premodern works of intolerance like the *Protocols* dogmatically rejected and it would be the cruelest irony if Jews should define themselves by the perspectives of those they should obviously oppose. As dangerous as the conflict between Israel and its neighboring states might be for Jews, which heightening of religious and nationalist zealotry only intensifies, just as dangerous is the constitutional battle in Israel taking place between the proponents of religious orthodoxy and secular life.

Calls from radicals for the abolition of religion are, of course, as abstract as they always have been. There is no program, no practice, no agent, and no serious ethical justification for such an enterprise. Modernity may project the erosion of rigidly organized belief systems and the type of spiritual life dominant in earlier times, but religious issues remain of crucial concern to millions upon millions of people. The liberal state must protect both the religious rights of the individual and the ability to make use of them. It can do so, however, only if each religion is understood as a private interest without any privileged claims to truth applicable to others of a different persuasion. Religious belief and a communitarian sense of belonging become authoritarian and dogmatic whenever they spill over into political life or, putting it another way, whenever private passions become identified with the public good. Such a situation is precisely what a constitutional order seeks to avoid and what the fanatic seeks to introduce.

Universal rights were the weapons with which Jews traditionally sought to combat their oppression. The affirmation of identity was never enough; it was always a question of the institutional terms in which it was recognized. The fight against antisemitism involves more than an insistence upon particularism. It also places primacy on the principles and the institutions through which conflicts between particular groups or individuals will be resolved. Increasingly the question for the state of Israel is whether it will privilege its commitment to liberal secular values or retreat into a new form of theocracy with a democratic veneer. There was nothing romantic about the *shtetl* and dogmatism is inherent in any form of religious messianism. Liberal society not only constrained the antisemite but helped Jews civilize themselves; it alone made the peaceful adjudication of their grievances possible.

Liberalism is an inherently secular theory and it always projected an assault on the ghetto: the more exemplary Israeli democracy becomes, in other words, the less *Jewish* it will be. Integration is the historical hallmark of the liberal idea: it is now a matter of integrating the *other*, the Palestinian or the Arab, in Israel as surely as it was a matter of integrating the person of color in the United States. The zealots sense the danger: they fear testing the salience of their convictions without the use of coercive institutions or dogmatic methods. Their ideological strategy is clear: proponents of an intolerant orthodoxy will transform religion into a reflex response against the freedom offered by modern secular life, while their chauvinistic allies will use the notions surrounding Jewish identity to exclude non-Jews from public life. The *illiberal* society predicated on the exercise of arbitrary power and prejudice is, unfortunately, not a thing of the past.

Jews have other political traditions upon which they can build. They derive from figures like Mendelssohn and Heine, Marx and Luxemburg, Blum and Einstein, Isaiah Berlin and Yitzhak Rabin. All of them understood the value of the liberal rule of law. Their cosmopolitanism contested the prevailing parochialism, and they considered the unfolding of individual potential as the loftiest aim toward which a society can strive. Their principles are unambiguously libertarian and progressive. Indeed, especially when compared with those of the zealots, their values stand in sharp contrast to those advocated by works like the *Protocols*.

The genuine struggle against antisemitism is ultimately no different than the genuine struggle against any other form of discrimination. It does not privilege the particular suffering of any group and it does not unconsciously embrace the values of its enemies. It instead places primacy upon a certain form of ethical conduct and a stance that *explicitly* speaks to the freedom of all minorities. Those who preach the particular without reference to the universal and who place faith above reason in political life, whatever their religion or race, remain mired in the past. Whether consciously or unconsciously, purposely or unintentionally, they are still ensnared in the grip of works like the *Protocols*. They will have learned nothing from the dire warning provided by Moses in the Old Testament: "Accursed is he who misleads the blind." (Deut 27:18).

NOTES

CHAPTER 2:
ANTISEMITISM FOR POPULAR CONSUMPTION

1. The pamphlet exists in many versions. An excellent annotated edition appeared in German edited by Jeffrey Sammons, *Die Protokolle der Weisen von Zion: Die Grundlage des modernen Antisemitismus—eine Fälschung. Text und Kommentar* (Gottingen: Wallstein Verlag, 1998). The selections here are taken from the *Protocols of the Learned Elders of Zion,* trans. Victor E. Marsden (London: Briton Publishing Society, 1923). Italics and capitalization are used as in Marsden's translation.

CHAPTER 3:
THE TEXT IN CONTEXT

1. References to the *Protocols* as reprinted in the previous chapter appear in square brackets for the convenience of the reader.

2. Léon Poliakov, *The History of Antisemitism: From Voltaire to Wagner,* trans. Miriam Kochan (New York: Vanguard Press, 1975), 38.

3. M. I. Roztovzeff, *Social and Economic History of the Hellenistic World* (Oxford: Clarendon Press, 1941).

4. Peter Schaeffer, *Judeophobia: Attitudes Toward the Jews in the Ancient World* (Cambridge: Harvard University Press, 1998).

5. Albert S. Lindemann, *Esau's Tears: Modern Anti-Semitism and the Rise of the Jews* (New York: Cambridge University Press, 1977), 3ff.

6. Emmanuel Levinas, *In the Time of the Nations,* trans. Michael B. Smith (Bloomington: Indiana University Press, 1994), 58.

7. Chaim Potok, *Wanderings: History of the Jews* (New York: Fawcett Crest, 1978), 40.

8. Ernest L. Abel, *The Roots of Antisemitism* (Cranbury, N.J.: Associated University Presses, 1975), 18.

9. Aristotle, *The Politics,* ed. and trans. Ernest Barker (New York: Oxford University Press, 1971), 6.

10. Erich Fromm, *Das jüdische Gesetz: Zur Soziologie des Diaspora-Judentums* (1922) ed. Rainer Funk und Bernd Sahler (Basel: Beltz, 1989).

11. Abel, *Roots of Antisemitism,* 50.

12. Note the excellent discussion by Burton Mack, *Who Wrote the New Testament?* (San Francisco: Harper, 1989), chaps. 1-2.

13. Robert Funk, Roy Hoover, and the Jesus Seminar, *The Five Gospels* (San Francisco: Harper, 1993), 533-37 has a roster of participants. The official findings of the seminar were that 82 percent of the words ascribed to Jesus in the New Testament were not spoken by him (p. 5). The seminar then engaged in separating what they described as Jesus as a "historical figure" from the transcendent "Christ of faith." While there is a lack of conclusive evidence to support that the former existed at all, there is a wealth of historical, literary, and theological scholarship about the true origins and folkloric traditions behind the accounts given in the synoptic Gospels attributed to Matthew, Mark, and Luke, as well as the book of John.

14. Mack, *Who Wrote the New Testament?,* 80-84.

15. Ibid., 139.

16. Ibid., 152.

17. Ibid., 170-71.

18. Elaine Pagels, *The Origin of Satan* (New York: Vintage, 1995), xx.

19. John Dominic Crossan, *Who Killed Jesus? Exposing the Roots of Anti-Semitism in the Gospel Story of the Death of Jesus* (San Francisco: HarperCollins, 1993).

20. John Shelby Spong, *Liberating the Gospels: Reading the Bible with Jewish Eyes* (San Francisco: Harper Collins, 1996), 272.

21. Detlev Claussen, *Vom Judenhass zum Antisemitismus: Materialien einer verleugneten Geschichte* (Darmstadt: Luchterhand, 1987), 18, 20-21.

22. Abel, *Roots of Antisemitism,* 10.

23. Helen Ellerbe, *The Dark Side of Christianity* (San Rafael, Cal.: Morningstar Books, 1995), 80

24. Henry Kamen, *The Spanish Inquisition: A Historical Revision* (New Haven: Yale University Press, 1998).

25. Martin Luther, "Preface to the Epistle of St. Paul to the Romans" in *Martin Luther: Selections from His Writings,* ed. John Dillenberger (New York: Doubleday, 1961), 26

26. James Shapiro, *Shakespeare and the Jews* (New York: Columbia University Press; 1997).

27. Stefan Rohrbacher and Michael Schmidt, *Judenbilder: Kulturgeschichte antijüdischer Mythen und antisemitischer Vorurteile* (Reinbek bei Hamburg: Rowohlt, 1991), 131-136; Aribert Schroeder, *Vampirismus: Seine Entwicklung vom Thema zum Motiv* (Frankfurt am Main: Akademische Verlagsanstalt, 1973).

28. "A Conspiracy to Take Over the World?—Wow!" on http://www.iahushua.com/ BeWise/july95.html.

29. Poliakov, *History of Antisemitism,* 458.

30. Ibid., 13; Blandine Kriegel, *The State and the Rule of Law,* trans. Marc A. LePain and Jeffrey C. Cohen (Princeton: Princeton University Press, 1994), 11ff., passim.

31. William O. MacCagg Jr., *A History of the Habsburg Jews, 1670-1918* (Bloomington: Indiana University Press, 1992), 27ff.

32. The classic text pleading for emancipation of the Jews in Germany is by Christian von Dohm, *Über die bürgerliche Verbesserung der Juden* (Hildesheim/New York: Olms, 1973).

33. Ulrich K. Preuss, *Constitutional Revolution: The Link Between Constitutionalism and Progress,* trans. Deborah Lucas Schneider (Atlantic Highlands, N.J.: Humanities Press International, 1995).

34. "The Christians' age-old disgust had communicated a sort of explosive charge to the very word 'Jew.' Even in enlightened circles, the name, with its emotive power, served as a standard of evil by virtue of custom. . . . Thus although more and more voices were raised on behalf of the Jew as a *man* in this period, defenders and detractors alike abided by the same meaning of the word. The Jew was therefore only esteemed on condition that he was not a Jew: a semantic ambiguity which was to make its contribution to the everlasting quality of modern anti-Semitism." Poliakov, *History of Antisemitism,* 55. Also Jacob Katz, *From Prejudice to Destruction: Anti-Semitism, 1700-1933* (Cambridge: Harvard University Press, 1980), 7ff., passim.

35. Pierre Manent, *An Intellectual History of Liberalism,* trans. Rebecca Balinski (Princeton: Princeton University Press, 1994), 21ff.

36. George L. Mosse, "The Jews and the Civic Religion of Nationalism," in *Confronting the Nation: Jewish and Western Nationalism* (Hanover, Mass.: Brandeis University Press, 1993), 121ff.

37. Cited in Katz, *From Prejudice to Destruction,* 56.

38. Eva G. Reichmann, *Hostages of Civilisation: The Sources of National Socialist Antisemitism* (Westport, Conn.: Greenwood Press, 1949), 20ff., passim.

39. Helmuth Plessner, *Die Verspätete Nation* (Stuttgart: W. Kohlhammer, 1959).

40. Fritz Stern, *The Failure of Illiberalism: Essays on the Political Culture of Modern Germany* (Chicago: University of Chicago Press, 1955), 3ff.

41. Reinhard Rürup, "Judenemanzipation und bürgerliche Gesellschaft in Deutschland" in *Vorurteil und Völkermord: Entwicklungslinien des Antisemitismus* eds. Wolfgang Benz and Werner Bergmann (Freiburg: Herder, 1997), 138.

42. For a nuanced interpretation, see Henry Pachter, "Marx and the Jews," in *Socialism in History: Political Essays,* ed. Stephen Eric Bronner (New York: Columbia University Press, 1984), 219-55.

43. Note the classic study by Paul W. Massing, *Rehearsal for Destruction: A Study of Political Antisemitism in Imperial Germany* (New York: Howard Fertig, 1967), 3ff., passim.

44. Reichmann, *Hostages of Civilisation,* 83ff.

45. Cited by Sir Isaiah Berlin, "Joseph de Maistre and the Origins of Fascism" in *The Crooked Timber of Humanity* (New York: Vintage Books, 1992), 100.

46. Cf. Kwame Anthony Appiah, "Cosmopolitan Patriots" in *Cosmopolitics: Thinking and Feeling Beyond the Nation,* eds. Peng Cheah and Bruce Robbins (Minneapolis: University of Minnesota Press, 1998), 111.

47. Katz, *From Prejudice to Destruction,* 61.

48. Thomas Nipperdey, *Deutsche Geschichte, 1866-1918: Machtstaat vor der Demokratie* (Munich: C. H. Beck Verlag, 1992), 291ff.

49. "Hep-hep" was an antisemitic cry or slogan that often accompanied antisemitic actions. Its roots are unclear although the best guess is that it goes back to the time of ancient Rome when the Temple fell and the Romans yelled "*Hierosolyma est perdita*" ("Jerusalem is lost"). Claussen, *Vom Judenhass zu Antisemitismus,* 74ff.

50. Priscilla Robertson, *Revolutions of 1848: A Social History* (Princeton: Princeton University Press, 1952).

51. John W. Boyer, *Political Radicalism in Late Imperial Vienna: Origins of the Christian Social Movement* (Chicago: University of Chicago, 1981).

52. Brigitte Hamann, *Hitlers Wien: Lehrjahre eines Diktators* (Munich: Piper Verlag, 1998), 337ff.

53. Peter G. J. Pulzer, *The Rise of Political Anti-Semitism in Germany and Austria* (New York: John Wiley, 1964).

54. Hamann, *Hitlers Wien,* 147ff.

55. Moshe Zimmermann, *Wilhelm Marr: The Patriarch of Anti-Semitism* (Oxford: Oxford University Press, 1986).

56. Jack Jacobs, "Friedrich Engels and 'the Jewish Question' Reconsidered" in *MEGA*-Studien 2 (1998): 1-21.

57. Note for a concise explanation of this difficult concept, Jürgen Habermas, "The Public Sphere: An Encyclopedia Article," in *Critical Theory and Society: A Reader,* eds. Stephen Eric Bronner and Douglas Kellner (New York: Routledge, 1989), 136ff.

58. Saul Friedländer, *Nazi Germany and the Jews: The Years of Persecution, 1933-1939* (New York: Harper Perennial, 1997), 75ff.

59. Jean-Denis Bredin, *The Affair: The Case of Alfred Dreyfus,* trans. Jeffrey Nehlman (New York: George Braziller, 1986).

60. Poliakov, *History of Antisemitism,* 24.

CHAPTER 4:
THE TALE OF A FORGERY

1. A fine collection of the various introduction, commentaries, and secondary material relevant to the *Protocols* is provided by Pierre-André Taguieff, *Les Protocols des Sages de Sion,* 2 vols. (Paris, 1992), 2:472ff.

2. Norman Cohn, *Europe's Inner Demons: An Inquiry Inspired by the Great Witch-Hunt* (New York: Basic Books, 1975).

3. Lucien Wolf, *The Myth of the Jewish Menace in World Affairs: The Truth About the Forged Protocols of the Elders of Zion* (New York: Macmillan, 1921), 8ff.

4. Norman Cohn, *Warrant for Genocide: The Myth of the Jewish World-Conspiracy and the Protocols of the Elders of Zion* (London: Eyre and Spottiswoode, 1967), 31.

5. Ibid., 32ff.

6. Nikolaus Markow, *Der Kampf der dunklen Mächte: Historischen Übersicht über die menschenfeindliche Tätigkeit des Judentums, vor allem in Russland,* trans. W. Klingelhofer (Frankfurt am Main: Welt-Dienst Verlag, 1944), 51.

7. Binjamin W. Segel, *A Lie and a Libel: The History of the* "Protocols of the Elders of Zion (1926)," trans. and ed. Richard S. Levy (Lincoln: University of Nebraska Press, 1993), 53.

8. Cohn, *Warrant for Genocide,* 53ff.

9. Hans Rogger, *Jewish Policies and Right-Wing Politics in Imperial Russia* (Berkeley: University of California Press), 22.

10. Armand du Chayla, "Sergey Alexandrovitch Nilus et les Protocols des Sages de Sion (1909-1920)," in *La Tribune Juive* (May 14, 1921). Translation in the archives of the American Jewish Committee (Protocols ab), 3ff. Note also the fine discussion by Michael Hagemeister, "Sergei Nilus und die "Protokolle der Weisen von Zion:" Überlegungen zur Forschungslage" in *Jahrbuch für Antisemitismusforschung* 5 (Frankfurt: Campus Verlag, 1992), 133ff.

11. Hadassah Ben-Itto, *"Die Protokolle der Weisen von Zion": Der Mythos der jüdischen Weltverschwörung: Anatomie einer Fälschung* (Berlin: Aufbau Verlag, 1998), 113.

12. Hagemeister, "Sergei Nilus und die "Protokolle der Weisen von Zion," 136ff.

13. Sigmund Livingston, *Protocols of the Wise Men of Zion* (New York: Educational Commission of the B'Nai Brith, 1945), 8.

14. Cohn, *Warrant for Genocide*, 68ff.

15. Leslie Fry, *Waters Flowing Eastward: The War Against the Kingship of Christ,* ed. and rev. by Rev. Denis Fahey (New Orleans: Flander Hull Publishing Co., 1988 ed.), 37ff.

16. "The Truth About the Protocols: A Literary Forgery," *The Times* (London), 16, 17, 18 August 1921, 18.

17. Ben-Itto, *Die Protokolle der Weisen von Zion,* 101-109.

18. Ibid., 121-29.

19. Fry, *Waters Flowing Eastward,* 73ff.

20. Herman Bernstein, *The Truth about "The Protocols of Zion:" A Complete Exposure* (1935) (New York: Ktav Publishing House, 1971), 32.

21. *Die Protokolle der Weisen von Zion: Das Weltoberungsprogramm der Juden,* (Berlin: Institut für Antisemitismusforschung, Technische Universität Berlin, ca. 1940).

22. Chayla, "Sergei Alexandrovich Nilus et les Protocols des Sages de Sion," 7.

23. Umberto Eco, "Eine Fiktion, die zum Alptraum wird: Die Protokolle der Weisen von Zion und ihre Entstehung" in *Frankfurter Allgemeine Zeitung* 2.7 (1994), s. B2ff.

24. Ben-Itto, *"Die Protokolle der Weisen von Zion,"* 50.

25. Cohn, *Warrant for Genocide,* 32ff.

26. Hermann Goedsche, *Biarritz* (Munich: Deutsche Volkverlag, 1933).

27. Note the discussion by Jeffrey Sammons, *Die Protokolle der Weisen von Zion—eine Fälschung. Text und Kommentar* (Göttingen: Wallstein Verlag, 1998).

28. Bernstein, *The Truth about "The Protocols,"* 22-23.

29. Benjamin W. Segel, *A Lie and a Libel,* 95ff.

30. "The Protocols of the Elders of Zion: Its History and Current Revival" in *Bulletin* No. 5-A (1933), The American Jewish Committee Library, 3ff. Also see *Die Protokollen der Weisen von Zion* (1998), 10, 21.

31. H. De Vries de Heekelingen, *Les Protocoles des Sages de Sion: Constituent-ils un Faux?* (Lausanne: Imprimere A. Rochat-Pache, 1938), 4.

32. Unwilling or unable to deal with the character of the forgery, or the connection between the *Protocols* with other antisemitic tracts, the *Protocols* have even recently been interpreted as an authentic, original program of the Freemasons. Note the section dealing with the *Protocols* in Michael Baigent, Richard Leigh, and Henry Lincoln, *The Holy Blood and the Holy Grail* (New York: Delacorte Press, 1982).

33. Walter Creuz, "*Les Protocols des Sages de Sion:* Leur Authenticité," in *Les Protocoles des Sages de Sion.* (Berlin: Institut für Antisemtisimusforschung, Technische Universität Berlin, 1978), 9-10.

34. Ben-Itto, *Die Protokolle der Weisen von Zion,* 221ff.

35. For a comparison of the texts in French, see Pierre Charles, S. J., "Les Protocols des Sages de Sion," in Taguieff, *Les Protocols des Sages de Sion,* 2:11ff.

36. Cited in Segel, *A Lie and a Libel,* 100-101.

37. Cohn, *Warrant for Genocide,* 74ff.

38. Ibid., 78.

39. Ibid., 106.

40. Hans-Dietrich Löwe, *The Tsars and the Jews: Reform, Reaction, and Antisemitism in Imperial Russia, 1772-1917* (New York: Harwood Academic Publishers, 1993), 46.

41. Rogger, *Jewish Policies and Right-Wing Politics in Imperial Russia,* 22-23.

42. A. Linden, "Die permanente Pogrom gegen die russichen Juden (1882-1903)," in *Die Juden-Pogrome in Russland,* published in Auftrag des Zionistischen Hilfsfonds in London von der zur Erforschung der Pogrome eingesetzten Kommission 2 Bde. (Köln-Leipzig, 1910), 99-133ff.

43. Bernstein, *The Truth about "The Protocols of Zion,"* 27-28.

44. John Gwyer, *Portraits of Mean Men: A Short History of the* Protocols of the Elders of Zion (London: Cobden-Sanderson, 1938), 77ff.

45. Robert Neumann, "Protokolle," in *Tribune* 9: 34 (1970): 3635ff.

46. Livingston, *Protocols of the Wise Men of Zion,* 4.

47. Ben-Itto, *Die Protokolle der Weisen von Zion,* 54ff.

48. A case in point is the popular reception given to the self-serving *The Last Diary of Tsarita Alexandra,* ed. Vladimir A. Kozlov and Vladimir M. Khrustalev (New Haven: Yale University Press, 1997). A relatively rare critical portrait of the royal couple is offered in the study by Brian Moynahan, *Rasputin: The Saint Who Sinned* (New York: Random House, 1997).

49. Löwe, *The Tsars and the Jews,* 222.

50. Ben-Itto, *Die Protokolle der Weisen von Zion,* 53.

51. Robert S. Wistrich, *Antisemitism: The Longest Hatred* (New York: Pantheon, 1991), 173.

52. Edward H. Judge, *Easter in Kishinev: Anatomy of a Pogrom* (New York: New York University Press, 1992).

53. Cited in Rev. Elias Newman, *The Fundamentalists' Resuscitation of the Antisemitic Protocol Forgery,* in ders. *The Protocols of the Elders of Zion: A Forgery* (Minneapolis, 1934), 19. An early account of the horrible fate suffered by many victims of these pogroms, particularly in Kishinev, is provided by Michael Davitt, *Within the Pale* (New York: A. S. Barnes, 1908).

54. Salo W. Baron, *The Russian Jew Under Tsars and Soviets* (New York: Macmillan, 1987), 61.

55. Maurice Samuel, *Blood Accusation: The Strange History of the Beiliss Case* (New York: Knopf, 1966).

56. Immanuel Geiss, *Der Lange Weg in die Katastrophe: Die Vorgeschichte des ersten Weltkriegs, 1815-1915* (Munich: Piper Verlag, 1990).

57. Felix Gilbert, *The End of the European Era, 1890 to the Present* (New York: W. W. Norton, 1979), 106; Paul Kennedy, *The Rise of the Anglo-German Antagonism* (London: Ashfield Press, 1980), 105ff., 2-37, 157-223.

58. Gilbert, *The End of the European Era,* 15.

59. Stephen Eric Bronner, *Moments of Decision: Political History and the Crises of Radicalism* (New York: Routledge, 1992), 21, passim.

60. John C. G. Rohl "Kaiser Wilhelm II und der deutsche Antisemitismus" in *Vorurteil und Völkermord: Entwicklungslinien des Antisemitismus,* eds. Wolfgang Benz and Werner Bergmann (Freiburg: Herder, 1997), 264.

61. Binjamin W. Segel, *A Lie and a Libel,* 59.

62. An interview with Henry Ford in the *New York World,* February 17, 1921.

63. Helmut Berding, "Der Aufstieg des Antisemitismus im Ersten Weltkreig," in *Vorurteil und Völkermord,* 288.

CHAPTER 5:
SPREADING THE NEWS

1. Stephen Eric Bronner, *Moments of Decision: Political History and the Crises of Radicalism* (New York: Routledge, 1992), 13ff.

2. Pierre Charles, S.J., "The Learned Elders of Zion" from *The Bridge: A Yearbook of Judaeo-Christian Studies* (New York: Pantheon, 1955), 1: 164.

3. Georges Sorel, *Reflections on Violence,* trans. T. W. Hulme and J. Roth (New York: Collier Books, 1950), 124ff.

4. Otto Ernst Schueddekopf, *Linke Leute von Rechts: National Bolsschwismus in Deutschland von 1918 bis 1933* (Stuttgart: Kohlhammer, 1960), 89.

5. Note the second volume in the magisterial work by Leszek Kolakowsi, *Main Currents of Marxism,* 3 vols., trans. P. S. Falla (New York: Oxford University Press, 1978).

6. Albert S. Lindemann, *Esau's Tears: Modern Antisemitism and the Rise of the Jews* (New York: Cambridge University Press, 1997), 175ff.

7. Saul Friedländer, *Nazi Germany and the Jews: The Years of Persecution, 1933-1939* (New York: Harper Perennial, 1992), 106ff.

8. George L. Mosse, *Confronting the Nation: Jewish and Western Nationalism* (Hanover, Mass.: Brandeis University Press, 1993), 7.

9. Rosa Luxemburg, "The Russian Revolution" in *Rosa Luxemburg Speaks,* ed. Mary-Alice Waters (New York: Pathfinder, 1970), 387-95.

10. Nikolaus Markow, *Der Kampf der dunklen Mächte: Jahr 1 u. Ztr. Bis 1917: Historische Übersicht über die menschenfeindliche Tätigkeit des Judentums, vor allem in Russland* übersetzt von W. Klingelhoefer (Frankfurt am Main: Welt-Dienst Verlag, 1944).

11. Lucien Wolf, *The Myth of the Jewish Menace in World Affairs: The Truth About the Forged Protocols of the Elders of Zion* (New York: Macmillan, 1921), 36.

12. Cohn, *Warrant for Genocide: The Myth of the Jewish World-Conspiracy and the Protocols of the Elders of Zion* (London: Eyre & Spottiswoode, 1967), 116-17

13. Alexander Borschtschagowski, *Orden fur einen Mord: Die Judenverfolgung unter Stalin* (Berlin: Propylaen, 1997).

14. "One of my friends told me this characteristic anecdote: He was in Kiev during the fighting. . . . He escaped in disguise, but was later arrested by the [White] soldiers of Petlioura who mistook him for a Jew and wished to shoot him. One of the chiefs whom he asked the reason for this said:

'You wish to give us a king with a head of gold. So it was stated at the sessions of your Wise Men of Zion.'" Chayla, "Sergey Alexandrovitch Nilus et le Protocols des Sages de Sion" in *La Tribune Juive,* 9.

15. Neumann, "Protokolle," in *Tribune 9:34* (1970): 3637.

16. Cited in Cohn, *Warrant for Genocide,* 124.

17. Agatha Christie, *The Big Four* (New York: Berkeley Books, 1984 ed.), 100, passim.

18. Stephen Eric Bronner, "Persistent Memories: Jewish Activists and the German Revolution of 1919," *New Politics* 5, 2 (Winter 1995): 83-94.

19. There is a huge literature on the Weimar Republic, but perhaps the most politically incisive rendering of events is still provided in the classic study by Arthur Rosenberg, *Geschichte der Weimarer Republik* (Mannheim: Europäische Verlagsanstalt, 1961).

20. Helmut Berding, "Der Aufsteig des Antisemitismus im Ersten Welt-krieg," in *Vorurteil und Völkermord: Entwicklungslinien des Antisemitis-mus,* ed. Wolfgang Benz and Werner Bergmann (Freidburg: Herder, 1997), 286.

21. Helmuth Plessner, *Die Verspätete Nation* (Stuttgart: Kohlhammer, 1959).

22. Mosse, "Community in the Thought of Nationalism, Fascism, and the Radical Right," in *Confronting the Nation,* 42.

23. Note the expanded discussion in Stephen Eric Bronner, *Ideas in Action: Political Tradition in the Twentieth Century* (Lanham, Md.: Rowman & Littlefield, 1999) 108ff.

24. Gerhard Czermak, *Christen Gegen Juden: Geschichte eines Verfolgung* (Reinbek bei Hamburg: Rowohlt, 1997), 167ff.

25. Paul J. Kingston, *Antisemitism in France During the 1930s: Organisations, Personalities and Propaganda* (North Umberside: University of Hull Press, 1983), 66.

26. Note the letter of 26 June 1946 in Hannah Arendt and Karl Jaspers, *Briefwechsel 1926-1969,* ed. by Lotte Kohler und Hans Saner (Munich: Piper, 1985), 81ff.

27. Daniel J. Goldhagen, *Hitler's Willing Executioners: Ordinary Germans and the Holocaust* (New York: Alfred Knopf, 1996).

28. Note the biographical sketch by Joachim Fest, "Alfred Rosenberg—The Forgotten Disciple," in *The Face of the Third Reich: Portraits of the Nazi Leadership,* trans. Michael Bullock (New York: Pantheon Books, 1970), 163ff.

29. Konrad Heiden, *Der Führer: Hitler's Rise to Power,* trans. Ralph Mann-nheim (Boston: Beacon, 1944), 4.

30. Werner Masur, *Der Sturm auf die Republik: Frühgeschichte der NSDAP* (Düsseldorf: Econ Verlag, 1994), 148-52.

31. Walter Laqueur, *Deutschland und Russland* (Berlin: Ullstein, 1966), 99-121.

32. Charles Bracelen Flood, *Hitler: The Path to Power* (Boston: Houghton Mifflin, 1989), 132.

33. Lucy S. Davidowicz, *The War Against the Jews 1933-1945* (New York: Holt, Rinehart & Winston, 1975), 71.

34. Rathenau also served as the model for the main character in the great novel, *The Man without Qualities,* by Robert Musil. On the extraordinary life of the former foreign minister, see Count Harry Kessler, *Walther Rathenau: His Life and Work* (New York: Harcourt, 1930).

35. Martin Sabrow, *Der Rathenaumord: Rekonstruktion einer Verschwörung gegen die Republik von Weimar* (Munich: Piper, 1994).

36. David Carroll, *French Literary Fascism: Nationalism, Anti-Semitism, and the Ideology of Culture* (Princeton: Princeton University Press, 1995).

37. Albert S. Lindemann, *The Jew Accused: Three Anti-Semitic Affairs (Dreyfus, Beiliss, Frank) 1894-1915* (Cambridge: Cambridge University Press, 1991), 277.

38. Gerhard Czermak, *Christen Gegen Juden,* 165ff.

39. David G. Goodman and Masanori Miyazawa, *Jews in the Japanese Mind: The History and Uses of a Cultural Stereotype* (New York: Free Press, 1995), 76ff.

40. Note the discussion regarding the South African version, which maintained that the Talmud and Torah commanded Jews to make non-Jews drink their urine and eat their vomit, by Hadassah Ben-Itto, *Die Protokolle der Weisen von Zion* (Berlin: Aufbau Verlag, 1998), 260ff.

41. The tale of the oath goes back to the *Rütlischwur* in 1291 when representatives of the three forest communities in Uri, Schwyz, and Unterwalden are said to have sworn to eternal unity. Hence the official name of Switzerland is still the "Swiss Confederation" *(Schweizerische Eidgenossenschaft)*. Note the famous play, *Wilhelm Tell,* by Friedrich Schiller, in which this event is described.

42. This trial serves as the framework for Ben-Itto's study, *Die Protokolle der Weisen von Zion,* to which the following discussion is indebted; 226ff, passim.

43. A pamphlet claiming that the trial actually proved the assertions made by the defendants about the Jews was published by Karl Bergmeister, *Der jüdische Weltverschwörungsplan: Die Protokolle der Weissen von Zion vor dem Strafgerichte in Bern* (1937). (First postwar edition, September 1977,

distributed by Liverpool, West Virginia: White Power Publications, 1977).

44. Ibid., 370.

45. Ernst Bloch, *Erbschaft dieser Zeit* (Frankfurt am Main: Suhrkamp, 1973), 65.

46. Hannah Arendt, *The Origins of Totalitarianism* (Cleveland: Meridian, 1958), 7

47. Ibid., 358.

48. Cohn, *Warrant for Genocide,* 194ff.

49. Friedländer, *Nazi Germany and the Jews,* 266ff, passim.

50. Stephen Eric Bronner, "Making Sense of Hell: Three Meditations on the Holocaust," *Political Studies* 47, 2 (June, 1999): 314-28.

51. Cf. Saul Friedländer, *Nazi Germany and the Jews,* 87.

52. Joachim Köhler, *Wagner's Hitler: Der Prophet und sein Vollstrecker* (Munich: Karl Blessing Verlag, 1997).

53. Cohn, *Warrant for Genocide,* 193.

54. Franz Alfred Six, *Freimaurer und Judenemanzipation* (Hamburg: Hanseatische Verlag, 1938).

55. Cited in Ernst Nolte, *Three Faces of Fascism: Action Français, Italian Fascism, National Socialism,* trans. L. Vennewitz (New York: Holt, Rhinehardt, Winston, 1965), 459.

56. Arendt, *Origins of Totalitarianism,* 358-60.

CHAPTER 6:
THE LEGACY OF A LIE

1. Note the research report, "The Post-War Career of the *Protocols of Zion,*" undertaken in London for the Institute of Jewish Affairs (December, 1981), No. 15 and by Marian Mushkat, "A Hoax Revived: On World Control by the 'Elders of Zion' and the Concept of Judeo-Communism," *International Problems* xxv (1986): 37ff.

2. Deborah E. Lipstadt, *Denying the Holocaust: The Growing Assault on Truth and Memory* (New York: Plume, 1993).

3. Jean-Francois Lyotard, *The Postmodern Condition: A Report on Knowledge,* trans. Geoff Bennington and Brian Massumi (Minneapolis: University of Minnesota Press, 1989).

4. Jodi Dean, *Aliens in America: Conspiracy Cultures from Outerspace to Cyberspace* (Ithaca, New York: Cornell University Press, 1998).

5. Note the discussion in "Conspiracy Prime" on http://www.netizen.org/archive/overv.htm.

6. Note the discussion of an unsuccessful secret plan devised between 1934 and 1940 that would have brought over a million Jews to Japan, in Marvin Tokayer and Mary Swartz, *The Fugu Plan: The Untold Story of the Japanese and the Jews During World War II* (New York: Paddington Press, 1979). Even in the absence of a grand plan, however, Japan was lenient to Jewish refugees and, by the time World War II began, Shanghai sheltered about 18,000. "The Japanese seem to have been moved by their distrust of Germany and possibly by humane considerations, but undoubtedly too . . . by their belief in Jewish power—a belief reinforced by Nazi propaganda and by study of the *Protocols of the Elders of Zion.*" Saul Friedländer, *Nazi Germany and the Jews: The Years of Persecution, 1933-1939* (New York: HarperCollins, 1997), 303.

7. Judith Butler, *Excitable Speech: A Politics of the Performative* (New York: Routledge, 1997).

8. Ben-Itto, *"Die Protokolle der Weisen von Zion": Der Mythos der jüdischen Weltverschwörung: Anatomie einer Fälschung* (Berlin: Aufbau Verlag, 1998), 229.

9. Ibid., 11ff, passim.

10. Benjamin Ginsberg, *The Fatal Embrace: Jews and the State* (Chicago: University of Chicago, 1993), 224ff.

11. Max Horkheimer and Theodor W. Adorno, *Dialectic of Enlightenment*, trans. John Cumming (New York: Herder & Herder, 1972), 168.

12. Note the excellent discussion by Leonard Dinnerstein, *Antisemitism in America* (New York: Oxford University Press, 1994), 228ff, 245ff.

13. See the list of Arabic translations provided by Yehoshafat Harkabi, *Arab Attitudes Toward Israel* (New York: Hart Publishing Co., 1971). Also note the interpretive article by Sylvia G. Haim, "A Muslim View of the 'Protocols,'" written for the American Jewish Committee (August 21, 1967).

14. Daniel Pipes, *The Hidden Hand: Middle East Fears of Conspiracy* (New York: St. Martin's Press, 1998), 309ff, passim.

15. I am much indebted for this discussion to the work of Diana Judd, "The Virtual Conspiracy: *The Protocols of the Elders of Zion* and the Internet" (unpublished paper).

16. http://webreview.com/nov10/features/hate/anti2.html.

17. Note "Christians & Conspiracy Theories: A Call to Repentance" on http://www.acts17-11.com/conspire.html, p. 1 of 13.

18. "Antisemitism: World Report 1997" prepared by the Institute for Jewish Policy Research and the American Jewish Committee at http://www.ort.org/jpr/AWRweb/ mainfeatures.htm, p. 8 of 12.

19. Robert S. Wistrich, *Antisemitism: The Longest Hatred* (New York: Pantheon, 1991), xxv.

20. Richard Hofstadter, *The Paranoid Style in American Politics and Other Essays* (Chicago: University of Chicago, 1979), 29.

21. Note, for example, the positions on evidence expressed in "Our View": www.thewinds.org/arc_editorial/ government/protocols_or_zion03-98.html, 3 of 6; "A combination of notes from *Smyrna,* the courageous Elizabeth Dilling, BeWISE, and The WORD.":www.pixi.com/%7Ebewise/newlight/html, p. 1 of 13.

22. Karl Marx, "The Eighteenth Brumaire of Louis Bonaparte" in Karl Marx and Frederick Engels, *Selected Works* (Moscow: Progress Publishers, 1969) 1:398.

23. Karl Marx and Frederick Engels, "Manifesto of the Communist Party" in *Selected Works,* 1:119.

24. Jeffrey M. Bale, "'Conspiracy Theories' and Clandestine Politics" on http://www.knowledge.co.uk/xxx/lobster/articles/129consp.htm, p. 2 of 6.

25. Max Weber, *The Protestant Ethic and the Spirit of Capitalism,* trans. Talcott Parsons (New York: Scribners, 1958).

26. Ernst Bloch, *Erbschaft dieser Zeit* (Frankfurt am Main: Suhrkamp, 1973 ed.), 111ff.

27. Jean-Paul Sartre, *Antisemite and Jew,* trans. George J. Becker (New York: Schocken, 1948), 27-28.

28. Hofstadter, *Paranoid Style in American Politics,* 36.

29. Note the discussion in Eric J. Hobsbawm, *Primitive Rebels: Studies in Archaic Forms of Social Movement in the 19th and 20th Centuries* (New York: Pantheon), 105-106.

30. Horkheimer and Adorno, *Dialectic of Enlightenment,* 172.

31. Friedländer, *Nazi Germany and the Jews,* 100.

32. Rev. Elias Newman, "The Fundamentalists' Resuscitation of the Anti-Semitic Protocol Forgery," in *The Protocols of the Elders of Zion: A Forgery* (Minneapolis, 1934), 4.

33. "Conspiracy! An Editorial" on http://www.the winds.org/arc_editorials/government/conspiracy6-97.html, p. 3 of 4.

34. Ulrich Beck, *Risk Society: Towards a New Modernity,* trans. Mark Ritter (London: Sage Publications, 1992), 127ff.

35. Dinnerstein, *Antisemitism in America,* 197ff.

36. Arthur Hertzberg, "The Graying of American Jewry," in *Jewish Polemics* (New York: Columbia University Press, 1992), 134.

37. A fine introduction to the issues involved is provided by Ian S. Lustick, "Israel's Dangerous Fundamentalists," *Foreign Policy* 68 (Fall 1967): 118ff.

38. Alan M. Dershowitz, *The Vanishing Jew: In Search of Jewish Identity for the Next Century* (Boston: Little Brown, 1997). Also note the cover story by Craig Horowitz, "Are American Jews Disappearing?," in *New York* (14 July 1997), 30ff.

39. Hertzberg, "Sharing Culture: Learning to Talk Together as Jews," in *Jewish Polemics,* 153-56.

40. Michael Goldberg, *Why Should Jews Survive?: Looking Past the Holocaust Toward a Jewish Future* (New York: Oxford University Press, 1995), 168.

41. Martin Buber, *Ich und Du* (Berlin: Schocken, 1922).

42. Emmanuel Levinas, *In the Time of the Nations,* trans. Michael B. Smith (Bloomington: Indiana University Press, 1994), 60.

43. Lustick, "Israel's Dangerous Fundamentalists," 123.

INDEX